This is a remarkable memoir, two memoirs really. One chronicles Larry Smith's odyssey from son of a mill town worker to accomplished teacher, writer, publisher, family man. We see a young man take his first uncertain steps from a way of life that had defined his family for generations. As he and wife Ann move from their beloved Ohio Valley, we also see the values of hard work, honesty, community and acceptance of others, instilled from his parents, impelling his life forward from college graduate to high school teacher to college professor. Throughout, love of family remains at the center of his life.

The other memoir is his creative odyssey. Shared is the evolution of his creative self as reflected in selections from his poetry, fiction, and biographies. It brings him—and us—to a precipice of understanding that is deep and profound, a spiritual and holistic view grounded in the world of nature and others.

The Thick of Thin is a joy to read and contemplate. Larry Smith has learned and accomplished much in his years which he generously shares here.

—Kurt Landefeld, author of *Jack's Memoir: Off the Road*

Mingo Junction, Ohio, photo by Andrew Borowiec

On Larry Smith's Fiction Writing:

"I like *Beyond Rust* and find it very affecting—Good, strong language, and a big heart shining through." –Sy Safransky

"Smith's skill as a poet enables him to develop through compelling imagery in *Working It Out* a man's search for and finding that he has the courage and self-acceptance needed to stand by the people he loves and to make a good life for himself and his family." –Edwina Pendarvis

On *Faces and Voices: Tales*

"After you read these stories, you will take a closer look at the waitress who refills your coffee, the man who cashes your check at the bank, the couple in the car that passes you on the secondary highway. What these monologues, letter and phone calls share is an urgency; with only the bare truth to guide them, Smith's characters struggle to make some sense in the world, and through telling their stories, they succeed." –Bonnie Jo Campbell

On *The Free Farm: Novel*

"Written in a strong, sensitive but never sentimentalizing voice, Smith has penned a kind of spiritual being-of-age novel, while still providing a clear-eyed look at a turbulent, fascinating era of the American experience." –Charles Dodd White

On Larry Smith's Memoir Writing

"'The Company of Widows,' [included in *Milldust and Roses*] one of the strongest pieces, describes a visit 'home' to his mother. It is homage to his parents, to the legacy of work 'as fabric of life,' and to working-class struggle that 'toughens you or it breaks your heart.'" –Janet Zandy

"Such a sweet, kind, modest, touching, an unassuming book...It is this simple pride in being 'common' that most touches me....I envy Smith this rooted, honest, and unabashedly loving portrait of his native land." –David Budbill

"This beautiful memoir of that part of the steel-hearted Midwest, by a writer who understands the poetry and poverty of the working-class poor, is something to be put in the hands of anyone unfamiliar with the history of steel towns, America's blue collar culture, and how it shaped lives and souls." –Norbert Blei

On Larry Smith's Poetry Writing

On *Steel Valley: Postcards & Letters*

"Smith lets us overhear the private griefs and joys of immigrants old and new, of millwrights, coal miners; victims of the Shadyside, Ohio floods; of college students; Vietnam-era expatriates; of mothers, wives, and union women in what becomes a kind of chorus of working-class America. Smith stands on back stoops and front porches reading over the shoulders of folk caught up in the paradoxes of Americans 'so lost and at home with their lives.'" –Richard Hague

On *Thoreau's Lost Journal*

"These poems are crisp, lucid, exact. They keep one hand always in contact with the earth, the other on the skin....I am moved by all of them: the regard for work, for tools, for the turns of phrase, for the legacy of sayings and skills." –Scott Russell Sanders

On *A River Remains: Poems*

"These poems look straight at the things we are most afraid of, and treats them with tenderness. Their speaker maintains a permeability to the human and nonhuman worlds that admits extremes of love and fear, body and soul, and still yet holds the center. This book is a lesson in saying yes to life." –Diane Gilliam Fisher

On *each moment all: Poems*

"Larry Smith writes of life's constant and precious things— sunrises, birds, gardens, breakfasts, dogs, fornt porches, and back yards. Teachers and poets, Parents and children. Those things that do not go away. Here is the conscious realization of them together as one in a personal matrix as simple and pure as the music of the moon." –mark s. kuhar

On *Lake Winds: Poems*

"Larry Smith takes a hard-eyed look at he suffering human beings cause one another and the inequalities of the world we live in. And yet these poems take the full measure of human life, finding the peace and humor that reside in family, in love, and in those smallest, ordinary moments of each lived day and the way their casual, unforced grace help us to live our lives." –Robert Cording

Other Books by Larry Smith

Fiction:
> *The Free Farm: A Novel* (Bottom Dog Press, 2011).
> *The Long River Home: A Novel* (Bottom Dog Press, 2009).
> *Faces and Voices: Tales* (Bird Dog Publishing, 2007).
> *Working It Out* (Ridgeway Press, 1998).
> *Beyond Rust* (Bottom Dog Press, 1995).

Memoirs:
> *Milldust and Roses* (Ridgeway Press, 2002).

Poetry:
> *Lake Winds: Poems* (Bottom Dog Press, 2014).
> *each moment all: Poems* (March Street Press, 2011).
> *Tu Fu Comes to America: A Story in Poems* (March Street Press 2010).
> *A River Remains* (WordTech Editions, 2006).
> *Thoreau's Lost Journal* (Westron Press 2002).
> *Steel Valley: Postcards & Letters* (Pig Iron Press, 1992).
> *Across These States* (Bottom Dog Press, 1985).
> *Scissors, Paper, Rock* (Cleveland State University Poetry Center, 1982).
> *Echo Without Sound: Poems by Larry Smith, Etchings by Stephen Smigocki* (Northwood Press, 1981).
> *Growth: Poems* (Northwood Press, (1975).

Biography:
> *Images of America: Mingo Junction,* co-edited with Guy Mason (Arcadia Publishing, 2011).
> *Lawrence Ferlinghetti: Poet-At-Large* (Southern Illinois University Press, 1983).
> *Kenneth Patchen: Rebel Poet in America* (A Consortium of Small Presses, 2000; rev. 2013).

Films (co-produced with Tom Koba):
> *James Wright's Ohio* (1988).
> *Kenneth Patchen: An Art of Engagement* (1989).

Bottom Dog Press

The Thick of Thin

Memoirs of a Working-Class Writer

Larry Smith

Harmony Memoir Series
Bottom Dog Press
Huron, Ohio

© 2017 Larry Smith
& Bottom Dog Press, Inc.
ISBN 978-0-933087-75-0

Credits
Cover Photo: Larry Smith
Photo page 3 by Andrew Borowiec
Author Photo (back cover) by Brian Smith
Cover Design: Susanna Sharp-Schwacke
Interior Photos from the Smith Family
and from Brian Smith
Acknowledgments

We thank the following for quotes from Emily Dickinson, "I'm Nobody" *Collected Poems* (Barnes & Noble Classics 2003); Henry David Thoreau from *Walden*; Kenneth Patchen, "The Orange Bears: Childhood in an Ohio Steeltown" *Collected Poems* (New Directions Publishing 1968); Wendell Berry, "The Peace of Wild Things" *Collected Poems* (North Point Press 1987); David Budbill, "The Ubiquitous Day Lily of July" on *Writer's Almanac* (online, Sept. 2013); Sue Monk Kidd in *Why We Write About Ourselves: Twenty Memoirists on Why They Expose Themselves (and Others) in the Name of Literature*, ed. Meredith Marin (Plume 2016).

The many selections of the author's writing are noted in the text, and his list of publications open this book.

I wish to thank all of the folks who helped me live then write about this life-story of mine, mostly my wife Ann who has shared most of it, but also for my close family of parents, brother, sisters, aunts, uncles, and children. And, of course, for the many teachers I had in and out of school. Most of my writing has been a paying back to the town of Mingo Junction, Ohio, in which I was born and raised in a working-class family. I thank fellow writers Ingrid Swanberg, Kurt Landefeld, Joel Rudinger, Susanna Sharp-Schwacke and Jim Daniels for their sharp editing and encouragement. This includes the members of the Firelands Writing Center. One's motives for writing are always complex, but I hope you sense my dedication to people and place.

Dedication

In my first book I wrote the simple dedication:

"For my family—all of you."

I repeat that here with a special appreciation
to my wife Ann, who has shared my life and dreams.

Author's Preface: The Circle Unbroken

At 73, I find myself on a spiritual retreat through the New Mexico desert communities of the native Pueblo people. The bus and walking tour with 40 fellow pilgrims is led by Richard Groves, director of my wife's Sacred Art of Living and Dying group. My hair, what's left of it, is gray, and my arm is still sore from shoulder surgery two months ago. My good wife Ann, with her own surgery for back pain, is seated beside me, and we half joke-half pray over the ancient healing site of Chimayo visited a day ago. We have sweated and hobbled along these ancient paths following Richard's lead, hearing his talks on history and tales of spiritual presence. I am a half-believer in the mysticism which these fellow travelers seem to embrace, but I know the power of belief and have witnessed it in the sacred work of Ann and others. Their being close with those struggling to embrace dying as a part of living is inspiring.

As I lean my head back against the bus seat, I look out at a desert landscape under bright sun. The rock formations and gorges are as different from our Ohio flatlands as one can imagine. Here was once an ocean bottom; back home we have the scarred flatland of ancient glaciers ending south in rocky hill lands. In the cool drift of the bus, I close my eyes and sense myself as a place, my life and its places written upon and through me. My youth in a working-class steel mill town in the Ohio Valley, my college life in the rolling hills of Southern Ohio, married life along the lake land suburb of Cleveland, then on to the rolling hills of Kent, Ohio, where we began to raise our daughter and witnessed the violent shootings of our students. In our mid-twenties, we sought the safety of small town life again, trading our Ohio River for the shore lands of Lake Erie in Huron, Ohio. Here Ann practiced and taught nursing, and I, after 40 years of teaching college English courses, would retire with the gold plated clock. During a sabbatical year, our young family of five journeyed to the ruggedly beautiful area of Sicily where we survived together and I learned far more than I taught at the university there. And here now in the arid desert of the Southwest I am seeking connection.

Clearly all of these places and times are deeply etched in us as we sit on this bus rolling through the American desert. Richard is preparing us for our experience of Bandelier National Parks Monument, near the Los Alamos site where the first atomic bombs were developed and tested and where the skies are still searched for signs of alien life. Bandelier is our final destination on this spiritual pilgrimage, site of the cliff dwellings of the Anasazi people from some 500-700 years ago, and a place that attracted such deep thinkers as Albert Einstein and Carl Jung. As the bus unloads, we don our hats and sun glasses, and take up our bottles of water against the hot sun. Passing through a modern visitor's center we follow a path over desert land. The gray-white cliffs rise out of this gorge, offering impressive formations of white volcanic ash on cliff sides.

Richard leads us to a site under a large cottonwood tree along the small Frijoles Creek. We have been twice warned by rangers to watch for tarantulas and rattle snakes, yet we circle out around this natural plant life serving as today's shrine. Richard blesses the site and passes a basket of blue corn flour and salt to touch and taste. Prayers ancient and modern are said to continue the rite of acceptance of all life and death as one. From the Tewa Indians we hear, "The great Circle of Life is a Circle of Unity with all things in the Universe including our Creator about which all life evolves. We are all equal in the circle. No one is in front of you, no one is behind you. No one is above you, and no one is below you. We are all equal in the circle of Life."

Richard steps forward holding the native made seed pod which we have been carrying. Raising it above his head, he suddenly crashes it upon the earth. We stare in silent wonder and are invited to gather a shard to take home with us along with our chosen stone. I have long let go chains of logic, dualism, and empirical reason on this pilgrimage to embrace this felt movement within, and so I welcome the tears at the corners of my eyes as we chant and then embrace.

Later as I climb the hillside path alone, sweating through sun and pain, I am able to mount the cliff walls and climb the primitive ladders in sun to enter the cool darkness of the dwellings and alcoves. A camera here would only be for others; the cliffs must be taken in like a deep breath. Breathe it…hold it…now release. Allow the light and darkness to mix. Just as we had been told that our special stone would find us, so these cliff dwellings pull me near as a place where I was and am meant to be. Again I sense it, how our path is not a destination but a converging movement toward our true self. I would trace mine for myself and you here.

*   *   *

A word about memoirs and this book's title. In launching into a book about oneself, one faces the question of worthiness: How is my life important enough to be of value to others? One can wrestle with this question for some time, putting off the huge task of actual writing until some realizations finally emerge. For me it's in the title "the thick of thin." Everyone has or is a story deserving of our listening, for everyone has a seed born into him or her that grows into a life of body and spirit. Mine doesn't seem to have high drama or tragic events, yet its commonality may be its chief virtue, its thickness. Another recurring concept, "converging paths," is from a realization that came while writing this, that the sense of our being resides in the many levels or planes of our existence. The symbol of the stacked rocks or cairn rose before me. We live on these intersecting planes—our work, our relationships, our sense of place (outer and inner), our spiritual awareness and growth, the things that matter over time.

Fortunately, as a writer, I've kept a record of my growth and can share it here, though my rocks may look more like books I've done. Chronology is a guide but simply as a map and not as vital of a record as our realizations and transformation. What we come to grasp and how we have changed are real keys here. Finally, memoir is what it implies—a recording of moments as memories. Not seeking agreement but striving for sincerity here, I share my humble life.

Part One

Converging Paths

"I should not talk so much about myself if there were anybody else whom I knew as well. Unfortunately, I am confined to this theme by the narrowness of my experience. Moreover, I, on my side, require of every writer, first or last, a simple and sincere account of his own life, and not merely what he has heard of other men's lives..."

–Henry David Thoreau

"At its best, writing draws from the inner life, from a place deep within where we are sourced. We could call it the life of the soul. This place is filled with so much genius—an ordinary genius that's common to us all. It's the room where our dreams and imagination live. It's where our wisdom lies, where memories are metabolized, images are born, and creative connections are made. I see it as an inner reservoir."

–Sue Monk Kidd

Chapter One: Born and Raised

"My life is not about me. I am about Life."
–Richard Rohr

I came into this world at 2 am on February 11th, my mother's birthday and a day before my father's. Mom, Jean Rae Putnam, was 20 years old, and Dad, Delbert Ross Smith, a day away from 22. In a week I would be home in Mingo Junction, where I might be lying in a white bassinet looking up at a woman in her flowered robe smiling down at me, perhaps singing, "Beautiful Brown Eyes," or she might be handing me into the strong hands of a man in a blue mill shirt. Perhaps a small boy, Davey, with a long face would be watching all of this, maybe waiting to pinch me when no one watches. Though the weather would be cold with snow blowing along the row of brick apartments, she might bundle me up, then dash the few feet over to an adjoining apartment where a young woman also in a bright robe would welcome her in. There another baby fairer than I (my lifelong friend Joy) would lie bundled on the couch. The woman, Mildred, would hug my mother and laugh, "Well, Jeanie, we did it. By God, what a trip it's been!" Both would laugh waking us babies, and we would answer them with cries to be fed...

Mom was still a young girl at 18 when she had brother David, yet she'd already begun learning the ways of being a grown-up wife and mother. I can still hear her humming as she worked about the little kitchen or sang on the porch at night with Dad. Her voice a soft cooing, his a deep rumble. Later Dad once said to her, "You sing like a school girl." And she said his voice was like a passing train. One of Dad's favorite stories, often told when Mom was not in the room, was of her packing his lunch pail one morning and filling his thermos with root beer soda pop. Knowing that he liked it, she wanted to please her hard working man. What she didn't know was that it would explode on the bus ride to work sending a stream of wetness gliding up the aisle and causing fellow passengers to stare back at the stream's fountainhead between his wet legs. Dad said that she cried when he first told her about it, but thereafter they both laughed. Though humble, theirs was a happy marriage with friends nearby and a front stoop for us children to play upon.

The apartment was perched high on North Hill overlooking the long Ohio River Valley in the rolling foothills of Appalachia. Brick and wooden houses built close together spread over the three hills of Mingo Junction. All looked down toward the long river where a roaring steel mill spread smoke and work over their town and lives. Loud trains hauling iron ore ran north and south along the river where long low coal barges seemed forever to be gliding up and down the valley. In those early years till I was four, I became the round faced, brown eyed kid, sometimes unfairly nicknamed as "pumpkin head," who always seemed to be looking out at the world in wonder.

It was those sepia colored Roosevelt years (born 1943 to be exact) with the country at war, and so at times the mill may have roared a little less as many of the men once working in the mills were off fighting in Europe and the Far East. At home, older men, those deemed unable to fight, and brave women kept the home fires burning making steel for ships and keeping families going. Fortunately for me, my own father was not taken. A freak football injury from high school had rendered his left arm mapped with enlarged blue-green veins, any of which once punctured could spell death. This didn't seem to matter in the steel mill where his work as brakeman on the railroad was fraught with risk. Work dangers seemed something we just lived with, like the radio reports of wartime battles elsewhere, including the Philippines where Uncle Harry was stationed. All news seemed to be quickly followed by happy swing tunes like the Andrews Sisters' "Boogie Woogie Bugle Boy," or "Don't Fence Me in."

By the time the war ended in 1945, Harry Truman was president and I was a toddler of two years, unaware of much more than my family, home, and the neighborhood kids from the porch stoop and yard. Certainly I was ignorant of the wounding and deaths, except to one close to home. My father's father, Ernie Smith, was killed in a mill accident when two railroad cars collided and crushed him. As a child I knew only that he was gone from our lives. Later I would learn that Wheeling Steel had offered Grandma $1,200 as compensation, or she could be paid a small monthly pension for the rest of her life. She wisely chose the latter and lived long—one form of revenge on the mills which were just beginning to take responsibility for workplace injuries and deaths.

I knew my grandfather Ernie Smith not at all. Only later would I hear of how he had come from his humble birthplace in McArthur, a poor town in rural Southern Ohio. Though only Ernie had lived in Southern Ohio, for years we Smiths spoke of the McArthur farm as "down home." The opposite of his irresponsible father, Andrew, young Ernie had taken the family reigns as provider. When the mines finally closed, Ernie and several brothers and a sister ventured north for jobs in industry. It was a forced migration but one the Smiths knuckled down to and dealt with. "We'll deal with it," seems our family motto, backed up with "We always have." As a youngster I would travel south with family to visit the Smith homestead in McArthur. Photos of me on horseback and propped on a tractor verify my presence there where we ate well, slept with family and learned to use their old wooden outhouse, a two-seater. I recall little more than this and an image of one large woman sitting on their back porch in a cane rocker smiling as she waved goodbye to us.

When Ernie first landed a job on the railroad in the Carnegie Steel Mill in Mingo Junction, he lived with his older brother Mont for a year, then he met Carrie, a country girl of German descent from a nearby coal mining area. The best story of their romance is one my Aunt Mary told us kids as we sat on their back porch one summer night while eating watermelon. It seems Ernie had borrowed a railroad hand-car to meet Carrie at a dance in nearby Cadiz, Ohio. They were both full of innocence and longing for connection. All went well for the love struck couple until Ernie on the way back at night was caught unaware. "Suddenly a train burst from a tunnel," Mary would say to our upturned faces, then throwing here arms wide, "And your grandpa had to leap wildly from the hand-car." Then she would laugh adding, "The old boy took a tumble on the rocky bank." We kids still stared up at her. "Oh, and he survived to marry your sweet grandmother here."

Grandma Carrie was a fine woman who spread good food and gentleness on me and anyone else who entered her comfortable home. She talked little and used such expressions as "yonder" and "quiet as church mice," which described herself, yet you knew you were loved in her warm home. The smell of fresh baked pies rose from her oven, pies that you knew would soon be placed fresh before you as she brushed back your hair with gentle hands worn smooth. Though she would live on till after I graduated from high school in 1961, during her last ten years, Carrie was slowly taken by a dementia that swallowed all of her words.

At times she took to "walking out," quietly slipping away from home till we noticed or received a neighbor's call and went running off to "find Grandma." I once asked my mother where Grandma might have been headed. Mom answered, "Oh, just out away from it all, I suppose. That woman's worked hard all her life." I do recall as a boy of eight, catching up with Grandma Carrie down on Commercial Street. Slipping my hand into hers, I slowly turned her around for the walk back home. She smiled down at me speaking the one word, "Deb," my father's name. Though the name was wrong, I remember thinking and knowing on our walk home that, I am me, Larry Smith, a person with a family and a town.

While little is known of Grandpa Ernie, except his strictness and tightness, in recent years, I've discovered how responsible he had to become with such a rambling father. His father Andrew somehow managed to have a wife in Ohio and another in West Virginia, and he kept a still and bootlegged, was a snake charmer for a time, and often abandoned the Ohio family for a month at a time leaving them to scrape together food from their garden or the nearby woods. One of his grandson's once told how people would say, "Given a dog, a wheelbarrow, and a shovel, old Andrew would scrape out a living from the hills." It was at best a subsistence living. Clearly Ernie sought to become the opposite of his father, guiding his family to some security and responsibility through strictness, yet I was pleased to learn that in his last decade my grandfather took into his home both his father Andrew and the parents of Carrie till their deaths in the 1930s. Great-grandfather Andrew, origins unknown, was a farm hand on the Eustler farm in McArthur till he married the German farmer's daughter, Mary Jane. As a presumed rebuke, they were given the single worst acre on the 100 acre Eustler farm.

While Ernie proved a stalwart of strictness and responsibility, Carrie was his counter-balance, earning the devotion of others through her big farm-girl heart and gentleness.

My mother's side of our family was even more of a puzzle, as I would begin to learn when at age four we moved in with her parents. Grandpa Raymond Putnam, who died of cancer when I was in high school, was a hard working Englishman from Weedsport, near Syracuse, New York. Proud of his craft as a rigger on the buildings and bridges of Pittsburgh, he would boast of such as he drove us through the city, declaring, "You see that. That's my building." "That's my bridge." For a time I came to believe that he owned most of the city. In 1945, a tragedy struck as they lost their eighteen-year-old son Dick to rheumatic heart disease. Then he and Grandmother Jean left the Ohio Valley and moved into a big farm house in remote Florence, Pennsylvania. This venture included my parents putting up half of the down payment, and moving all of us into the big gray house at the end of the road in rural Florence. He and Dad would drive the twenty miles to work together at Weirton Steel.

The move seems to have been an uneven venture from the start with my grandparents assuming the upstairs and basement, and our little family taking the single lower level. While my brother and I were free to roam the large yard and throw fallen apples to the cows in the field next door, we were forbidden to go into the basement where Grandpa kept his tools and workbench and where Grandmother kept her precious preserves. Our use of the single bathroom upstairs was also strictly monitored to prevent us from using up cistern water. Unable to flush, I would enjoy peeing apart the floating leaves of tobacco from Grandfather's pipe. The real tension, however, was between

Grandmother and her daughter, my mother, both named Jean. Though Mom had become pregnant by my father while still in high school, my father was such a solid provider and loving man, that Grandmother's resentment of him seemed unreal and certainly unearned. Of course as a kid, I couldn't be aware of the source of this, though all of us felt the tension; only later did I learn from Mom some of the back-story of our living in a house of unspoken grief and resentment. For me as a pre-schooler with a brother who went off to a one-room schoolhouse down the road, I grew close to my mother and would often catch her in tears of pain.

It might take a book to grasp my grandmother Jean Putnam for her wit, cunning, and often her meanness, but I'll sum up what I've come to understand. Her father Alexander Cochran came with his family to America from Scotland at age 13 already initiated in work as a coal miner in the town of Ayr, near poet Robert Burns' village in Ayershire County. In 1890 America working in the Allegheny coal mines at 24, Alexander met and married an eighteen-year-old Northern Irish girl, Charlotte Carson. Together they settled outside of Pittsburgh in McDonald, Pennsylvania, where he worked as a supervisor in the mines and later in real estate sales and as a justice of the peace. Together they raised a family of 11 children, my grandmother being the second, born in 1892.

I visited my Cochran great-grandparents a few times at family reunions and birthdays for Squire Alexander, as he was called. A strong yet quiet guy always with a pipe in his mouth and a bulldog at his feet, he once scared us kids with a story of the bear in the basement, keeping us from what my mother described on the ride home as "more beer than bear." It took a trip to Scotland with my wife Ann and my brother and his wife Joan to realize how very Scot the old man really was, as were my grandmother and mother. All three loved poetry and wrote light verse full of Scot wit and loved to kid.

Mom's joking or kidding seemed a way of taking life and making it tolerable. She used to call sweetly to us boys, "David...Larry...honey...come on down..." then switch tone entirely, "I want to smack you." And we would stop quick on the stairs, then all laugh. I think Mom was also my first fiction writing teacher, for she had a way of taking the facts of a story while reading in the newspaper, then still pretending to read, inflate it with imagination leading to absurdity and laughter. "DiCarlos Market on Commercial Street was the scene of a robbery on Thursday morning...the thieves blew a hole in the back wall and took off with the goods...Also six naked chickens are now on the loose."

Generally her joking was just good fun, but once she may have gone too far. After my brother's friend Hatcher had refused to listen to my mother telling him, "Hey, now please get your big feet off the sofa. And while I'm at it, do stay out of our refrigerator." When he ignored both and stole her precious fudge, she retaliated the next day by handing him some broken pieces of chocolate to eat on his way to school. "Go now," she said ushering him out the door, "Run along." And go he did when the Ex-Lax hit old Hatch and he got the runs for his bad behavior. This trick playing also came from her father, Raymond, who was known to play pranks on fellow workers in the mill, including tossing firecrackers into their lockers. While we lived in Florence with them, he used to come home late at night and announce his presence by rubbing his thumb stiffly up the front window making it rattle like a thunder storm, scaring us all. Then he would disappear, something he was good at.

That was the joking side, but there was also the Cochran silent treatment that Grandmother Jean would practice, where anger turned to a wicked sullenness that could last for weeks. My mother once said she was forced to be the go-between ("She said to tell you...." "He said to tell you....") for her mother and father for two weeks till everyone forgot what they had fought over. Once after we moved and were visiting them, we saw them face a tragic fire to their Florence house. Driving home from an ice cream stand in nearby Burgettstown, we followed fire trucks to their front yard. Hoses and ladders were running everywhere, yet no one was hurt, except Grandma's beloved canaries who died from the smoke. I'd never seen her cry like that for any of us. When the fire source was located as Grandpa's pipe in a sweater pocket, you can bet he paid for it in silence, which may have been better than her sharp tongued words.

This all was livable, except for how my mother's mother often rode Mom for her mistakes or her perceived weakness, thereby making her weaker still with a wounded self-image. I often think of my mother as having the Scot wit and the Irish insecurity. As we would drive to Florence for a rare visit, Mother would be coaching us strongly on our manners: "Now take only one piece of candy, and don't run around making noise in their presence." "For gosh sake, don't talk or get down from the table." And so we were more afraid than happy to be there, the opposite of Grandma Smith's home where we always felt welcome. Later in life we learned of Grandmother's trick of placing photos of daughter Charlotte's family about the house before we would arrive, and then of placing photos of us about when Charlotte came to visit. This was done not as a joke but as a rebuke for perceived neglect, and yet not a word was spoken of this to her.

The housing situation in Florence finally broke, and I had a part in it. While we were still living with my grandparents, my mother and father had gone off shopping and left me alone with Grandmother upstairs. I soon grew tired of playing with cars, my brother was off at school, and so when I heard her coming down the steps, I hid behind the door. She walked right in as always snooping a bit, and when I jumped out from behind the door calling out "Surprise!" she jumped, startled, then quickly countered me with a wicked face and the screeching words, "You sneaky boy! You are such a snake—just like your mother!" She then bolted in retreat. Later when I told this story to my mother, she trembled and her cheeks grew red, then she grew angry. That evening she had me repeat the telling of my story to my father, "You tell your father. Tell him just what you told me." I did and Dad was ready to storm upstairs and confront "the old battleax," a term I had never heard him use. Language calls to language.

"You see," said my mother. "You see what I'm up against living under her watch. Nothing is good enough for her. And here, she's gone and insulted your son and your wife as snakes." Even I at four could tell that if Mom wanted to calm Dad down, she was headed in the wrong direction. But then she added. "We've got to move out."

Dad offered no resistance to this. "Tillie [his pet name for her], I've watched this abuse for months and kept silent. It was a bad idea our coming here, but we had to give it a go." She took his hand, but he was not through. "You're what...six months along now. Let's hold on till the baby is born, then we are moving back home to my family and our friends in Mingo."

Wow, I thought as a kid, *My words can have real power.*

And so, soon after Mom delivered my sister Janis one stormy night in February, 1949, the Smiths packed up.

With a borrowed pick-up truck, Uncle Harry's help, and a car loaded with us and our toys, we headed back to our "home" in the Ohio Valley.

*   *   *

This might be a nice place to end this segment, only the story and the sadness of these estranged grandparents has lived on in me. Mom dearly loved them both, and yet neither seemed able to really love her or us back. I've come to see them as not bad people, only limited and cold. And I do have some happy memories with them: a bright clown suit made by Grandmother that has passed through the generations, a Pittsburgh Pirates season opener to which Grandfather Putnam took me, my brother and father. And there was a singular summer day when he sat with me on their front porch swing and told me his life story. Swinging back and forth staring up through the vine, I heard of a farm, horses, his father working jobs. But I was only nine and could not really take it all in, and sadly he never spoke of it again. I have wondered if this need for revelation came with his diagnosis then for cancer. Because of my youth and his reticence, he took his story to the grave.

As dear as my grandchildren are to Ann and me, as much as we are involved in their lives, my mother's parents simply were not present for us. Was it a sign of the times, of men and women working long hours to keep family alive yet becoming too tired to love and be with their children, or was it the result of their own lost childhood? Psychologist Carl G. Jung, puts it simply: "The greatest tragedy of the family is the unlived lives of the parents." Was this the wounding of losing a young son and being unable to mourn? And was this insecurity so nearly passed on to us, to me? In my mid-sixties I found myself seeking wholeness by writing a novel, *The Long River Home,* seeking in some way to project images and stories of my lost grandparents into my life.

Just as parents often raise families in reaction to their own parenting, so my parents Jean and Deb responded differently from theirs. My mother was a welcoming and funny person providing a place where her and our friends gathered. She read Dr. Benjamin Spock's *Baby and Child Care* book cover to cover when it came out in 1947, advocating a nurturing approach to family. If Dad worked hard to provide for us, Mom kept our sprits alive by giving us the humor to accept the struggle. My father was clearly there for us when he came home from work, taking us to church or guiding our Cub and Boy Scout troops, or later having us work alongside of him. Yet in letters found after my father's death, I learned that before my mother became pregnant with my brother David, he had made plans to go to Detroit and study to be a mechanic. Did Dad ever regret his choice to marry young as he labored long out in the weather checking the train's air brakes and throwing switches to make rent, car, and grocery payments? I don't know, but one thing I'm sure of is that my father and Ann's father, John, and millions of men raising families in the 1950's, changed that old life pattern of parental absence. They did this by showing up as a caring presence in their children's lives. For that heritage and model I am forever thankful.

Chapter Two: Family Moves & Early Schooling

The same year Charles Schulz created his "Peanuts" comic strip, I started school. While not exactly a Charlie Brown in 1949, I did carry a lot of innocence into that first overcrowded classroom as the war and post-war baby boom children entered school. I immediately lost some of that innocence when my precious Roy Rogers pencil box, with neat sliding drawer, colored pencils, compass, and eraser, was stolen the second day of school. *Poor pencil box, poor me.* Our class overflow was moved into a second first grade classroom with Mrs. Fithen, a sweet, clean, and caring woman who taught us order. Our school and classroom windows all faced downtown Mingo in the foreground and rising behind were the huge blast furnaces, cranes, and car dumper of the Wheeling Steel mill. The roar and clang of the mill, muted somewhat by the school's brick walls and thick windows, nevertheless entered our bodies. We lived in it, and it in us.

As I understand it now, the socialization role of schools in the 1950s was very much an indoctrination to social values and a training for moving upward from immigrant status and working-class norms. Older women as grade school teachers became our mentors in math and reading but also in manners. We learned to stand and wait our turn, and also to listen when others spoke. At the Smith home, graciousness and civility were given to us by my mother who cautioned us, "No, we do not say *yense* for *you* or *I seen something.*" "Listen when someone is speaking and do not interrupt." "Do not chew gum when you're on stage." And later I recall her cautioning me, "Never pull up to a girl's house and beep the horn for her." Finally her coverall maxim, "Good manners cost us nothing yet say much about who we are." Not so much afraid of social disgrace or seeking betterment, Mom wanted us to be able to do well wherever we were. And that's how we took it. My father's watchword for us was, "Do unto others as you'd have them do unto you," and "If you can't say something nice about someone, say nothing at all." As far as I can recall, he never spoke ill of anyone, not even my Grandmother Putnam, who continued to diminish him, despite all that he did for her and us. As I would discover, before my mother's surprise pregnancy, Dad's goal was to attend college or gain training as a mechanic. He quickly sacrificed that to marry and to eventually raise a family of four children. His goal for college was then transferred to my brother and me as Dad took on second jobs to enable us to be the first Smiths to enter and graduate from college. Were we living out his dreams? Clearly, but it had nothing to do with social status, and we both ended by taking up service careers in teaching.

Though we accepted the diversity of our working-class town with its ethnic baker and butcher shops, the Italian, Polish, and Slovak social drinking clubs and many European languages, it was in school that we experienced this diversity most. Here we shared desks with kids who were Black, or of Italian, Slovakian, Serbian, German, Irish, Polish, and Hungarian descent, to name only some. We ran with them in gym class, included girls in our playground games, and walked home together. From my kid's innocent view, there was no ethnic superiority scale, no class totem pole. Later I would hear stories of how in the 1930s my and Ann's grandfathers had each been contacted respectively by the Klan and the Mafia, but to a kid we were all equally working-class. Yes, there was some public racial divide. Though I had heard the melting pot image, I favored the fresh salad bowl of many peoples. We would witness this merging of culture in the grocery shops and at school and church, but most dramatically in watching our parents sit together with everyone else in the Mingo Show. Together they might receive a free plate or gravy boat on dish night or hold bingo cards for the Wednesday night coverall grand prize of $100. Without offense, I recall standing in line for the matinee and taking in the rich smells of foods on clothes and the music of other languages as young and old we stood waiting together.

There might be some separation by neighborhoods, but that was more due to family extension and to waves or chains of immigration to America than it was to forced restrictions of choice. The only real status signs I recall were how high up your house lay on the hill rising above the millyard. Eventually the lowest paid workers' homes were down in The Bottoms area surrounding the mill, then across the railroad tracks at the foot of Church, Reservoir, or North Hills where lay slightly better homes. Generally the further you climbed up the hill away from the smoke and noise of the mill, the bigger the houses, the better off were the families, but the gradations were slight and invisible to a young kid. Living proximity and intermarriage were already erasing much of the ethnocentric bias. My wife's mother broke the code as an Italian woman marrying a Hungarian man. I, a white Anglo-Saxon Presbyterian, would marry an Italian-Hungarian Catholic girl. Eventually we had religious and racial intermarriage. One story of these changing times comes from my wife's grandfather Caesar Ferroni. An immigrant laborer from Italy, he often told of the day his mill supervisor stopped him to question, "Why is it you damn dagos keep moving up on my hill?" His answer may have been just a gesture or a smile, but its message was simple, "Because we can."

When we returned from Florence to Mingo in 1949, our new home was Uncle Mont's rental house located halfway up the hill on Murdock Street, near the Church Hill playground. Because houses there are typically built on the deep sloping hillside, multiple floors are common. Enter from the ground floor back and you're at one level with the kitchen or basement; up a narrow stairway and you're at level two facing the street above with its living room and bedroom; up another level and you are "upstairs" with the bathroom and another bedroom or two. Though our yard was long, the house itself was squeezed up front into a narrow column. One of the legends was that a previous renter had been blown off the toilet seat by a stroke of lightning, something I never failed to think of while sitting there, especially during a storm. I also recall the vivid book covers of my parents' pulp mysteries stacked near the toilet for longer visits. Somehow the bathroom was the right place for the darker side and hints of the mystery of sex. The house's proximity to the playground, however, where neighbor kids gathered compensated for any faults in its layout. I was never lonely there, nor was my mother who had friends and neighbors to chat with at every turn.

The word "turn" holds a special meaning in the Ohio Valley, where it is used to indicate the working "shifts" or "turns" in the schedules that workers and their families were forced to adjust to: Exs. Shifts ran 8 to 4, 4 to 12, 12 to 8, etc. It was often a weekly rotation of mornings, afternoons, and night shifts that they performed and to which the family had to adjust. Worst was the midnight shift for the worker who returned home weary and with shades drawn and doors shut, tried to sleep during the day while the children kept the quiet. David and I faced either "Hush, your father's asleep" or "Quiet, don't wake the baby." The usual greeting when two workers met was "Where you workin'?" or "What shift you on?" Essentially work was the center of life in working-class families struggling to survive, and in most of the Ohio Valley that work was in three related industries—the steel mills, on the railroads, or in the mines—and so when a strike came along, everyone joined in and everyone hurt. But we "dealt with it," and survived in our worker homes and way of life with the help of family and with neighbors who not only knew you, but also helped you out....watching kids, sharing rides to the grocery stores, keeping track of stray pets and kids, walking with or driving you to church. The mom-and-pop stores on every block ran tabs because they knew and trusted you as neighbors. These communal values remained a part of us working-class kids.

One memory from that house was of my father buying these soft boxing gloves for us boys, 5 and 7, then his trying to teach us to box. It went okay until David landed a punch to my face causing my nose to bleed and me to cry out, thus ending my boxing career with one blow. Mom's scolding of Dad, "Just look what you've gone and done!" didn't earn me many points with him either. Nevertheless David and I continued to wrestle on the floor, most of the time ending with his sitting on my chest, his knees pinning my arms to the floor as I gasped, "Uncle." Never done in meanness, it became our way of playing and touching, at times coaxing Dad to join in. For it was brother David who really introduced me to things, especially to books and reading. Each Saturday before we went to the matinee at the Mingo Show, he would take me down to our town's library. Though only a storefront space on Commercial Street, it opened the world to me and others. And it was David who placed those books of history and sports heroes into my hands. Though the magic of films might take us to India or Indiana, those books did it with the beauty of words, an important lesson for me.

Then there was the incident of our sled riding down our steep front street done before the city trucks spread ashes to destroy our fun. On one memorable slide I ended with the bumper of a neighbor's car pressed fast against my chest, knocking the wind from my lungs. Lying there literally breathless in the snow and certain I was dying, I was resurrected by my brother shouting, "Get back. Leave him alone!" Then he bent down, slightly lifted me up by the belt and dropped me back down again to release and bring in my breath. He was my hero for a while after that. We were always close brothers, almost carbon copies until I began to break the mold away. People often said, "Oh, here comes David-and-Larry" as though it were one word, we one entity. When I hear the term "brotherly love," I still think of us two. Today when we meet up I call him "Mr. Responsibility." I'm not sure what he calls me.

One person I can't forget is pretty Shirley Mae who lived next door, a friend and girl I would take to my first dance six years later, someone I would hold a secret crush on for a decade. Pretty with blonde, curly hair, sparkling blue eyes, and a dimpled smile, Shirley and memories of her are yet tinged with sadness. One morning I found Mom in the kitchen gathering fresh bought fruit into a basket of oranges and apples and bananas, things we didn't see every day. When I reached for an orange, there was Mom's quick tap on the hand and "Ack...get your little mitts off of those. That's for Shirley Mae who's sick next door." I frowned while Mom handed me a banana and half explained, "Poor girl. She has it rough." That day she had the strep throat, and later I learned that Shirley's father was a step-dad, that her real father had died a couple years before. We walked to school together for years and played while watching her little brother Billy and my sister Janis dig in the yard between our houses.

Several years later the Boy Scout troop would hold a dance in the basement of the Methodist church, and it was Shirley whom I asked and who accepted. With I in a dress shirt and slacks and Shirley in a flowered skirt and white blouse, we entered the hall decorated with crepe paper streamers. We nodded shyly to friends and for a long while sat along the wall drinking too sweet punch until I braved asking her, "Would you like to dance with me?"

"Yes, of course," she answered, "I've been waiting." And so we took hands and moved slowly around the floor, finding our way into this wonderful thing called dancing. Mom had taught me the "two step," and for the first time on a slow dance I felt a girl in my arms—Shirley's back, yielding yet straight, her hair, soft and sweet, the closeness delicious. All time stopped, until our scout master called, "This is the last dance, kids," and I held her closer.

Shirley and I walked home, holding hands in the evening air, and I left her at her front door. Then in moonlight I literally flew down the street to home and my dreams. Shirley and I would go through all of our school years together, I admiring her for her smartness in the classroom, her genuine kindness to others, as well as for her natural beauty. As I grew older, Mom would hint more than once of Shirley's "rough life" at home, though Shirley never showed it. Though our paths would ultimately part, Shirley helped bring me into the world of boy-girl life and friendship.

The 1950s were the green Eisenhower years, a retired general and Republican who surprised our union town by bringing a stable and peaceful time to our world. By 1953 we had moved down the street closer to Grandma Smith, and into a nicer house. My mother had kept an eye on this rental house owned by Grandma Carrie, and despite my father's objections, had written to the older couple living there urging them to move on. And so, when I was in the third grade, we moved to 310 Murdock Street, a two-story house with three bedrooms, kitchen and pantry, a front and back porch, basement, and a garage at the end of a yard. In Mingo no one thought of their yard as a lawn. Hedges or a rickety fence might surround it, but it clearly was seen as one step away from a field to be used for play and leashless neighbors' dogs.

Again that year an unexpected overflow of students caused them to merge my 3rd grade class with a like group of 4th graders into Mrs. Brettell's split classroom. She was a friend of my mother and acted much like her. Laughing with us, she shared more than "taught." In her room I began to love birds and, by extension, nature, found up from the industrial valley into the nearby woodsy hills. Each week, our teacher would present a drawing of a bird for us to learn about, then color, usually while the 4th graders did their math or English.

A school practice that year, I swear it, was the Ivory Soap campaign for cleanliness. Sitting in rows, one student would rise and go down the row checking the others for clean nails, hands, neck, and teeth. It was an awful and awkward inspection we were subject to and forced to perform. If someone was found lacking, they were actually given a tiny bar of Ivory Soap that came with public disgrace. I remember sweating it out the day I had to be inspector because Petey was in our row, a boy who was poor and slow and also not clean. I did not want to give him that soap bar. And so, while others watched me, for the first time ever I dared to question a teacher and I openly refused. As we were beginning, I spoke, "Mrs. Brettell, I can't do this. I'm really sorry. It just feels wrong to do like this." A hush fell over the class as I prepared to have the world come crashing down on me. But then, Allen Merzi, a fourth grader and the principal's son, rose from his desk to say, "I agree, Mrs. B. It just ain't right."

To her lasting credit, our teacher paused, then smiled, "It just *isn't* right, Allen. And you know, children, I've been thinking this myself." We all stared at her as she added, "And so we won't tell anyone, but we just won't do this anymore. Okay?" We nodded, as she added, "Get out your bird drawings and we'll color instead." Amidst gasps and laughter, applause went up. I looked over at Allen and simply smiled, for again I had found my voice among others. Our words held weight in the world. From that day on, Mrs. B was high on my and everyone's list of favorite teachers.

Though a distant war began in Korea in 1950 as we entered school, another battle at home had more impact on our lives. The polio scare of the early 1950s affected every family, especially those with children. By 1952 poliomyelitis which often included paralysis, had affected 59,000 people in the U.S. including my good friend Billy Peeler. For two years after he returned home from the hospital, I walked down the alley to sit with him in his bedroom weaving lanyards, listening to music, and talking of sports and girls. I watched in awe as his parents placed hot packs on his limp legs and did slow exercises developed by Australia's Sister Elizabeth Kenny. Often I would look back at my friend lying there, and at night dream that I was him and he me. Parents at the time were in a near panic of losing us, and so we became somehow more precious as they followed advice of feeding us well and disciplining us to always keep clean and to stay out of crowds. There was no swimming those summers at the Mingo pool, and rare were the trips to the Mingo Show or playground. Though the March of Dimes campaign developed to fight back, the disease kept increasing, affecting the most frail and young.

And then in 1955, when my baby sister Debra Jean was born, word spread that a miraculous vaccine for polio had been developed by Dr. Jonas Salk (son of Polish Jewish immigrants) working nearby at the University of Pittsburgh School of Medicine. Tested for three years on a million people, it had shown dramatic results, and so a program of national inoculation began. Soon we school kids were marched down to the school office area where we were lined up in the hallway as the three town doctors, Dr. Albaugh, Dr. Riney, and Dr. Cava along with nurses and volunteers gave us shots of the vaccine. By 1957 Dr. Albert Sabin (a Polish immigrant) would develop an oral vaccine, but we took our shots bravely and hoped we would be set free of the disease, the fear, and our life restrictions.

By the time junior high school came along, on the second floor of the Central building, I was still finding my place among my classmates, my town, and the world. My school work was a little above average. My areas of excelling were minimal, and I was comfortable with that until one day six weeks into the school year, I watched as our home-room teacher went up to the corner chalk board and wrote the names of those on the Honor Roll. She would leave them there for a week, so those who made it could be proud, mostly girls, though there were a few guys, and my brother two years ahead of me was a regular. Shirley Mae was always on the honor roll, and so I decided I too would be. I began studying harder, asking questions in class, watching my scores on tests, and so the next time they wrote the names on the board, Larry Smith was one of them. Though this may seem a small thing, it represented a real growth, a new awareness and focus on learning and achievement that would last a lifetime. When I received the "Most Outstanding Boy" award upon graduating from eighth grade, I felt a certain rightness about myself. Yet I remember my friend Allen saying to me, "Boy, I thought it would be

Johnny McFarland." I didn't know how to respond to that, so I agreed with him, "Yeah, me too." My ego was not that strong, but neither was my resentment. However, this questioning of self-worth remained a part of me, as it does for many working-class folks.

Up until junior high my only achievement was in starting on the 6th grade basketball team. We played in the old sunken gym nicknamed "The Dungeon" for its smallness, high walls, and darkness. Here we also had gym classes. In the lower grades we marched around the gym in cake walks holding sweaty hands with the girls. But in sixth grade, only the boys took gym, while the girls stayed upstairs and did sewing and crafts. With the bell, we boys would run down the stairs to the locker room where we dressed in t-shirts and shorts, socks and gym shoes. But that meant we also undressed and took showers in front of each other. Up until then, that had only happened at the Mingo pool where everyone just dropped their jeans and already had swimsuits on, and no one forced you to take a shower. And so our pool dressing all happened quickly, except for those older boys who lingered at the high peep hole to the girls' locker room.

The gym locker room provided another place for a personal and social revelation. As I undressed and looked around, I saw for the first time how really poor some of my classmates were. Their underclothes, if they had them, were often worn to threads and unwashed—no real crime, but many of them also had not washed their young bodies in a long time. There were "high water marks" around their necks and low ones around their feet. But most moving were the scars and welts on some of their backs and buttocks where a parent's belt had obviously struck hard or often. I remember that "Coach," the gym teacher, would come in to force everyone into the showers. And I thought, *Well, he must see these marks and know where they came from. Why doesn't he say or do something? Why doesn't someone?* In fact, our gym class typically ended with one boy given a belt and chasing the rushing pack of us to smack someone on the ass or back, then pass the belt on as he went up to shower and the wild chase continued.

Not only was beating allowed, it was ingrained in us. Today it seems we were all being abused. My mother had no answer for me when I asked about the welts, for back in the 1950s, parental abuse was either given a nod or not spoken of. This silence around so obvious wounding and pain ate at me then as it does still today. Torn by feeling compassion for these my friends yet also feeling more fortunate than they, I've carried these images, conflicting emotions, and irrational guilt into adult life. Yet I do believe that witnessing how vulnerable life is can lead us to sensing how more precious and to be loved it is. The story of Siddhartha Buddha is one of his awakening to the pain in the world and growing compassion through it. Though I was no kid Buddha, I did find early empathy for others.

While this may sound a bit self-righteous, I assure you that I would not have been known as a crusader then, but I was waking to the wrong in the world, and the social situation of school was where it was happening. School proved a ground for testing things with my own behavior. In 5th grade when Tom, a boy in my class, kept pushing me on the playground, I finally pushed back and in a flash wrestled him to the ground and sat on his chest, my brother's style. In screams of "Fight...fight....fight on the playground!" Tom and I were suddenly surrounded by bored upperclassmen cheering us on. The playground had turned into an arena. While Tom refused to say "Uncle," the crowd was calling for me to "Sock him, man,...sock him in the face." I could not, and would not. My anger had long been appeased and we were both tired of it all. So when the warning bell rang to come into school, it acted as the end of our boxing round. We both rose, looked at each other, and walked into the building. I tasted blood from my lip where his ring-fisted hand had landed. Minutes later, we were proudly seated in Mrs. Dean's classroom, garnering the attention of all. We had briefly come out of the shadows. Then an older boy came into the room and told Mrs. Dean, "Smith and Thompson are to report with me to the Principal's Office." A hush went up as our reputation collapsed on the floor, and as we marched up the stairs, I'm sure we were both considering what punishment would fit our crime.

All knew that Principal Merzi handled every issue with the paddle, never far from his side. Jane, the secretary nodded to us and pointed towards a bench. And so we sat wordless in his outer office awaiting our fate. Too soon the door opened and out came Principal Merzi, the dreaded wooden paddle at his side. He gave me a half frown-half smile of recognition, for yes, he was my good friend Allen's father and he knew my parents. With his stub of a forefinger (blown off by a railroad blasting cap) we got our hard talking to, and a warning "Boys, if this happens again...," and as he smacked the paddle, we were given a week of expected detentions. Then we were made to shake hands and told to return to our classroom. That day I learned two things: that I did not like fighting and that knowing someone actually can pay off, as it did for me that rare time.

In Mrs. Schwab's 5th grade music class I did not fare as well. Here I received my first public punishment for laughing at the woman's selection of songs, "Buffalo Girls, Won't You Come Out Tonight." That was all it took for a silly kid and an insecure teacher: a laugh, a smirk, a rolling of the eyes at a command. "Rise at your seat, young man," her red face demanded of me. "Come forward and hold out your hands." Then she pulled out a silly wooden ruler. As I grinned while looking around at my friends for support in this absurdity, she instructed, "Now open and reverse your palms." My face said, *How much could this hurt!* But then she, redder faced now, also turned the ruler on its side so that the edge with the hidden metal strip was pointed down at my knuckles. One—two—three times it came down, stinging and leaving my knuckles bloody. My only victory that day was that I did not cry before my classmates, one of which was Shirley Mae. Later the dreaded Mrs. Schwab would strike again when Billy Peeler and I auditioned for a cornet duet in the school talent show. Her revenge arrived as she laughed out loud at our performance. "No way, boys. You just don't have it." Here was an older chubby woman laughing at two young boys and delighting in it. My revenge, afflicted upon myself, was that I put the cornet back in its case for two years. *That would show her*! Thankfully I reclaimed it in 7th grade, and by 8th grade I had earned a place in the high school marching band. Finally, in the school operetta while the whole cast sang the finale on stage, Mrs. Schwab, stopped the rehearsal to call out, "You there, Larry and Billy, just move your lips on this one. Don't sing." Despite all this persecution by a somewhat twisted adult teacher, music would remain my close friend all of my life.

Two other cases of my getting into trouble involved others. In fourth grade I started hanging around with the downtown boys from school. Freddy, Harry, Ronnie and I hung out on Saturdays, and this day we decided to hit the Mingo Five and Dime store. There was no need we faced, only the challenge to shoplift some small item from the counter. Two stole pens, another, a plastic wallet, and I, a small pair of useless shoe cleats. We escaped free and were laughing over our crime skills in front of Islay's store when I felt a hand grip firm on my shoulder. It was the Five and

Dime store owner who had been watching us, and as my friends scattered like mice, he boasted, "Don't worry. I've got you now, and I'm going to make an example of you." Why I asked was this all directed at me? Yet when the police chief showed up, I was soon spilling the beans and naming my co-partners in crime.

Once all the names were taken down along with phone numbers, I was released to walk home where I feared my friends might be waiting to beat me up, a fate I seemed to deserve. However, when they greeted me outside of Minnie's Store, it was with laughter and understanding. We would share the guilt and the newfound fame. Our sentence from the mayor was to serve a daily detention at the Mingo Police Station, a fate we learned to embrace as did the bored policemen who welcomed our company with cokes and pretzels. My father did not appreciate any of it, however, and after two weeks of detention asked the town mayor if we could be paroled. What hurt more than any whipping or public scolding was Dad's taking me aside and saying, "Boy, you have disgraced our family's good name. I hope you know that." I still wince when I remember this.

A fifth grade crime incident was tied to sports. Ronnie and I had decided we wanted to try out for high jump in track, and the only high jump pit was inside the school stadium. It was kept locked on weekends, and we should have left it that way, but all we wanted to do was use the track for its intended purpose. And so, early Saturday morning we climbed the fence as hundreds of others had done over the years. We ran a few laps, then long and high jumped for half an hour. Before we left we saw something was wrong. The window to the locker room was shattered and glass lay on the upper bleachers. We looked inside to see salt tablets scattered on the floor, paper programs tossed about. We had just turned and were getting out of there when Ronnie bumped my arm. "Oh my god, look." It was Freddy Staffalino the groundskeeper and town policeman running right for us. We made a quick dash for the fence row, but Freddy was there to grasp us by the neck as we ducked to slide under.

Again word spread that we had done the break-in, and so were each questioned by the school principal and track coach. Suspension was threatened. Our pleas of innocence were not heard till two weeks later when the real culprits confessed. By then we had already stolen any notoriety for the crime, and topping it, we got to enjoy the coach's public apology in gym class that week. Once again I had shown myself a broken shadow of my brother's fine example.

Lest I come over as a little rascal, I should clarify that I was also the boy delivering papers, running errands for my grandma and aunt, doing chores around the house, trying to be a good brother and son, attending Sunday school and church with my siblings each week, carrying out the mottos of the Cub and Boy Scouts, and beginning to earn good grades in school while also taking parts in the school plays. My breaking of rules, often misadventures, seems now to be my testing of who I was and who I was to be.

A most memorable time in my development came in junior high English with our teacher Mrs. Ruth Merzi. It was she who handed me a treasure and tool for life—poetry and writing. I had never been more than a casual reader at that point....mostly those sports profile books gotten from that town library. But that day in 6th grade English class, Mrs. Merzi calmed us down with the words, "Now students, I have a great gift for you." Our treat proved not to be cookies or her reading us a story, but a small closely printed pamphlet which she handed to each of us individually.

"These are given to you to keep. After we use them in class, they are yours." Our disappointment at not being handed a food treat disappeared in the importance she spread over us in those little books of poems. "Now people, we can thank Haldeman-Julius Printing for this gift," she said smiling over us. "They believe we all should share in the word and that poems can be like little prayers to life. Now who wants to read the poem 'I'm Nobody' on page four?" Shirley had her hand up and was chosen. We each read it once to ourselves, then she instructed Shirley, "Now read it nice and clear. Take your time, and treasure every word by Miss Emily Dickinson." With a clear sincere voice she read,

> I'm nobody! Who are you?
> Are you nobody, too?
> Then there's a pair of us--don't tell!
> They'd banish us, you know.
> How dreary to be somebody!
> How public, like a frog
> To tell your name the livelong day
> To an admiring bog!

I felt as though Shirley was speaking her life to us, declaring the views of others and her own quiet pride. We read these poems and carried the little books in our pockets or purses and willingly memorized a poem each week when the next booklets arrived. What is more, Mrs. Merzi asked us to write our own poems and to share them on Friday Poetry Day. Sometimes they were written on the board, but always read aloud. I loved it and her for opening the blinds on this window, one I would never close. I date this as the beginning of my life as a writer. I found Robert Frost here and Walt Whitman, and of course Emily Dickinson. And I heard the deeper thoughts of my classmates. Thinking back, I believe the idea of publishing books was also planted in me then. The family of Haldeman-Julius of Girard, Kansas, for decades would print the inexpensive Little Blue Books series of classic and liberal writings for all. This remained a model of publishing as an act of caring and sharing, one I hope to have carried on by editing and publishing the hundreds of Bottom Dog Press books.

During these junior high years of awakenings and transformations (1954-1957), my brother and I were taken on travel adventures by our bachelor uncle Harry, or Satch, as he was familiarly known. Like his father Ernie and his brother Deb, he worked 50 weeks of the year as a railroader in the steel mill, and, as though released on bail, went traveling the remaining two. From some generosity of the spirit, what now seems a love for us, Uncle Satch would take my brother and me with him to different regions of the country. We also went to Cleveland Indians games with him and Grandma Smith, for he was one of their greatest fans, keeping the game records on the brown paper wrappers of his *Esquire* magazines (which my brother and I would devour when we got older.) Not exactly a man of the world, Satch was quiet, shy, and introverted, and yet he extended himself to us and wanted our boy company. Often he would join in the play of the trip perhaps releasing his inner child through us. When we grew too old or otherwise interested in high school life, he would begin flying to rare parts of the world, indulging in that Smith family wanderlust. Once I asked my dad if he was ever jealous of Satch's bachelor travels, and he smiled and half-mockingly said, "But then I wouldn't have you kids."

We always drove on these trips in his new Chrysler or DeSoto cars, and our destinations were well planned with the aid of the American Auto Association trip guides and travel books of places to stay, eat, and see. My brother and I would peruse these on the long drives and hunt for a motel with a swimming pool. Satch never refused, and he paid for everything. One requirement was that we stay awake and be good company, and so we took turns being his co-pilot and navigator. On one long drive through Kansas, with the sun beating down on us and the flatlands, we both slept in the back seat and were awakened when Satch stopped the car and took on a soldier hitchhiker. We drove on, the two of us boys astonished and listening to Uncle Satch talk with this stranger. Later he told us, "Now that's what happens when you boys check out on me."

On one such trip we traveled to New England with my aunt Mary (his and Dad's sister) and Grandma Carrie. We stayed in an old boarding house on the coast at Marblehead while Mary stayed with her old friend from Washington D.C. On one trip to Florida, the tempers raised as Satch had one plan for the trip and Aunt Mary another. Those two lived together with Grandma and argued like husband and wife. On this trip to old St. Petersburg, David and I were searching for the fountain of youth, only to find that the trip was already over. "We're heading back," is all he said, and Aunt Mary just shrugged her shoulders and rolled her eyes.

Other trips with just the guys were out west to the Badlands and Mount Rushmore of the Dakotas, to the beautiful rugged West Coast and the redwoods of Muir Woods. The greatest trip, however, was with Uncle Satch and my father. We spent a week in Yellowstone National Park watching geysers and mud pits, riding horses, and sleeping in the rustic cabins near the lodge where we stoked our own fire and went to sleep listening to the cry of coyotes. My father and Satch were seen as brothers close up, not unlike David and me. Dad was a man of action and warmth, Satch a man of reading and withdrawal, but they listened to each other and shared the lead. Unknowingly David and I absorbed their lesson of understanding and caring for each other. Did the trips broaden us? Without a doubt; we had seen other parts of the world, but also other ways of living.

Our own nuclear family could not afford such travels, though we did load up the station wagon one hot summer and drove to visit my mother's girlhood friends in Lordsburg, New Mexico. We did not stay in AAA motels, but slept that first night crowded in the car. The next morning, my travel worn mother summed it all up in two words, "No more." "Enough" would have sufficed. The typical family vacation with my parents, sisters Janis and Debbie, and brother David and sometimes other Mingo friends was north to the shores of Lake Erie, ironically where I would spend my working days and the last 50 years of my life. As we would drive north up Route 7 from the Ohio Valley, we tortured our parents with the "Are we there yet?" refrain, then sang out when someone spotted water and called out, "Lake Erie! Lake Erie!" Here we would rent a small lake cottage for a week, spend our days on the tiny front deck or down on the beach and then crowd back in for sleep at night. We loved it, all of us sharing and having fun with our parents, without work hanging over their heads or ours. We found freedom at being in another place. I do recall one drive to a fancy restaurant in Vermilion where the hostess found a table for all six of us. "This is special," Mom said. Then we looked down at the menus, back to Mom, and Mom looked over at Dad. He looked around at us all, swallowed then calmly said, "Kids. We're leaving." We folded our menus on our plates and all rose to casually walk right out the front doors again. Our dinner that night was fish sandwiches and fries picked up at the local drive-thru and eaten under a moonlit sky on the cottage picnic tables above the beach. And no one complained.

Were we poor? Now, this seems the right place to introduce how poverty and class shaped my world and identity. I must admit that my brother and my sisters, and my wife and I disagree over whether we were indeed "poor" growing up. Poverty can be such a harsh word. David points out that our father always had work and paid the bills. I know that Ann's father labored in a steel mill as well, and yet she felt not at all "poor." We do agree that in our youth we didn't think about being poor. In thinking that we were all equal we may have also felt that we were all the same, and we were not. Our talks reveal that Ann's mother managed money much better than my folks and did not allow Ann or her sister Janet to see any strains over paying bills. I, on the other hand, recall my parents at the kitchen table struggling or arguing over bills and where the money would come from to pay them. Some mornings Mom would search desperately for sister Janis' school milk money, often hitting up David or me for change earned on our newspaper routes. I think the term "working poor" fits best for our condition and for all our family and friends. It is not something to be proud of or ashamed of. As they say in the Valley, "At least we eat good," and our expectations were realistic. While we always had enough to "get by," money or the absence of it could be palpably felt.

An incident I remember vividly when eight and in fifth grade was playing with Eddie. He lived down by the mill flats where I didn't often go. That day we ran around wildly, going up to the gates of the Nut-and-Washer plant behind his small house. When I asked if his dad worked there, he just said, "My dad's away." Okay, I didn't ask. When we grew hungry Eddie said, "Wait here," and went into his kitchen returning with two peanut butter sandwiches on some pretty dry bread. I didn't complain, because it tasted good sitting there on his front steps. Later our play brought us up to our backyard on Murdock Street. When we went inside for a glass of water, I recall Eddie saying, "Man, you have yourself a big house." I never thought of it that way, but nodded. Then we went back out to shoot some baskets. We could not get enough of each other that day. And then Mom came out on the back porch and called me over. "Dinner's ready," She said and softly, "Eddie's welcome to eat with us...just hot dogs and beans." I was so happy, but when I looked around, Eddie was gone. "What the heck!" I thought and called out his name several times. When I asked Mom about it, she said, "Oh, honey, nothing's wrong. Eddie just wasn't comfortable eating here." It took a long while for me to realize his embarrassment at feeling a have-not among the haves, even though we just wanted to share. Creeping up on me was the realization that though we were all equal, we were not all the same.

Later in a college Introduction to Sociology course I was introduced to the socio-economic view of class structure. The professor wrote across the board the levels of Lower, Middle, and Upper, then added their gradations of upper lower, lower middle, etc. Next he asked each of us to write down the class to which we thought we belonged. I imagine most of us at this Presbyterian liberal arts college wrote down some level of "middle." When he began to explain the class basis in education, income, and occupation type, I became a little nervous. Levels of each were given, years of schooling, specific incomes for the times, occupation types, and to my dismay I found myself placed in the lower level. I was relieved that he did not ask us to share that day, for I was clearly a working-class kid in a middle class school, one that ignored my own culture. Eventually I would learn to accept class as a condition and not a judgment of character, and eventually I found strength in the solidarity of my working-class self. I recall studying for the big exam and mentally rejecting such boxed in terminology as "the poor" and "upper" and "lower," and I soon switched from sociology to psychology as my minor, dealing with persons not groups. Whether we were "poor" or not was simply above judgment, for one thing I clearly knew—I did not have an unhappy childhood.

Chapter Three: High School Years

When I entered Mingo Central High School in 1957, I simply walked 20 yards from my elementary and junior high school into another brick building. And yet it was miles away in terms of social context. As a humble freshman low on the totem pole, my only claim to status was my having already played cornet in the high school marching band and my walking in the big footprints of my brother. Teachers often confused us calling me "David," instead of "Larry." David's friends who identified him by his middle name "Ross," referred to me as "Little Rossi." When I was younger, this did not bother me so much; we did resemble each other at 5' 11" with dark hair and slim body type. At home we watched the "Ozzie and Harriet Show" and saw ourselves as sons David (older and wiser) and Ricky (musician and joker). My own brother David was a good guy, and his was a fine shadow to stand in for a time. And yet, by behavior I was clearly seeking to stand in a new light. Though we both were quiet and thoughtful, and we knew how to work by delivering newspapers or helping Dad restore and build houses, David had never gotten into the school troubles that I had. While he played end on the football team, I played cornet in the marching band. While I started on the freshman basketball team, he dropped out to compete in intramurals. We each joined the school clubs where he was often an officer, I a mere pledge yet ready to rise through the ranks. Deeper than this, in our family I became the funny man, and he the straight shooter. Though this may sound like a rivalry, in fact we generally admired and helped each other, as we did our younger sisters at home.

While David was dating some junior girls, I was still sweating over asking a freshman girl on a date. This went back to an incident in junior high when as a sixth grade boy I was asked to a dance at the R&A Hall by an eighth grade girl. Darlene was a really pretty girl with beautiful eyes, ample breasts, and at least 4 inches height on me. I cleared it with my mom, and David offered a grunting "Yeah, she's okay." I was spun out of my mind with delight in being sought out by her or anyone. That night I dressed in black pants and a new pink shirt that David mocked, "Wow, really duding it up, brother."

I walked down the hill to pick up Darlene at her house in the Bottoms area. Her mom took my hand then cautioned me, "Now, you promise me you'll bring her home by 9 o'clock." "Yes, Ma'am, I will," I said, captured as I was in the aura of Darlene's beauty and sweet scent. It was raining lightly so I held the umbrella, which her mother had thrust into my hand, high above for Darlene. To my thrill, four times my arm brushed against her breast, which she somehow didn't seem to notice. She was nice, and we chatted of teachers and school, though she was clearly on another par than I. At the dance, she was grabbed by her friend Janie who whisked her aside for some private talk. I just looked around, beaming in my new status among eighth graders.

We danced a few times, and during one break we found ourselves standing beside my brother. He smiled at me then looked away, but Darlene took his hand and said, "Come on, brother David, let's dance this one." And they did a nice slow dance to the song "This I Swear" by the Skyliners, one of my favorites. Dateless that night, David seemed uncomfortable being around us and soon moved away.

Darlene was quickly joined by Janie who boldly asked, "Hey girl, how did it go? Did he dance real close?" Something was going on, and with their giggling a veil was slowly lifting from my eyes. Darlene had a crush on my big brother, and she was getting to him through me. What a sap I was. I tried to swallow, then excused myself to the boys' room to wash my face. My stature in the mirror had shrunken drastically.

And so when Darlene and her friends headed down to Isaly's where she had promised to buy me an ice cream sundae, not only did I refuse, but I told Darlene, "Thanks, but I see what's going on here. I'm a little stupid, but I'm not blind. I'm headed home. And, oh yeah, I am not my brother." She looked a little puzzled, but reached for my hand and smiled, "Okay, Larry. I understand, but I did have a nice time with you."

The walk up the hill to home was painful, as wordless and alone, I quickly passed the other kids from school, then took the alleyway. When I got home I lied to Mom saying, "Oh sure. I had a good time. It was fun," and then I headed up to my room. David was lying there on his bed listening to the Everly Brothers on his record player. "How was it, little brother?" he asked.

I turned and said, "Awful. She just asked me to get to you."

He didn't answer for a moment, then looked at my broken face just as the Everly's broke into "When Will I Be Loved." I swear it. "Well, yeah," he said touching my arm, "I could have told you that."

"Yeah," I sighed loudly, "You should have."

*   *   *

Thankfully high school did not live up to the threats we had heard: "Wait till you get to high school, you'll see. It's going to be much harder. You really have to work." Once one learned the building layout and the changing of classes, it was junior high all over again, except that now as freshmen we were beginners again in the social ranking. One thing I gradually picked up on was how you could easily be classified in high school: *He's a band geek…She's a party girl…He's a jock…She's a goody goody…He's a greaser or a rack. etc.* David's advice was good, "Stay out of boxes by crossing lines." And so, while I marched in the band, I also played basketball and ran track, and I did well in the classroom. Afterall, it was the age of Sputnik, 1957, when America awoke to Russia's power in launching the first satellite into space. This small sphere with four radio antenna circling the planet had Americans both fearful and jealous, resulting in a renewed emphasis on math and science in the schools which affected us all.

Again, I followed my brother's example of joining clubs: The Future Teachers of America and the Key Club; I wrote for the Min-Hi-Go school paper, and later was inducted into the National Honor Society. The FTA was a surprise to me, but in a small town like ours, teachers and nurses were the first line of professionals. And so, I began to know that I wanted to go to college, though I was not sure why. I was selected to the prestigious Key Club, a service group sponsored by the local Kiwanis Club. It brought me into contact with a 'key' person, Paul Sogan, business teacher, faculty advisor, and junior then varsity basketball coach. Somehow he instilled in us working-class boys a much needed sense of discipline and self-respect. He had us selling Easter candy door to door raising funds for charities, standing outside the Hub Department store in the frigid cold collecting for the Salvation Army, but also gathering once a week for a well run lunch meeting.

Most of all, he took us to state and national conventions dressed in suits and ties where we typically placed first awards in competition among the smaller clubs. And so our knowledge circle extended beyond Mingo to Columbus, Youngstown, and Cleveland, and eventually much further to Boston, Chicago, and even Toronto, Canada. We traveled to these conventions by buses, cars, and trains. Once there, we were given a schedule of meetings and set free to explore the city around our hotel. If we acted a fool, he would let us know, as would other members. At each place Sogan would wrangle a deal with a local restaurant for a fine dinner for us all. There's a slogan that, "You can take the boy out of the Valley, but you can't take the Valley out of the boy." Well, he managed to take us out and yet see the best Valley in us with pride in who we were wherever we were. This would help me survive at college, and later when my wife Ann and I moved up north to a Cleveland suburb where I taught in a school of 3,000, while also serving as—the Key Club advisor.

*   *   *

During my junior year another revelation occurred. I played on the reserve basketball team and like most, sat on the bench for the varsity games. In a turn of events while watching our senior team losing yet another game, I grew aroused and strangely focused. "I can do this," I kept thinking, and so when the coach finally sent me in, I was a regular fireball of enthusiasm. I was razzing the other team, stealing the ball, passing it off under the basket, and our team and I rose from the ashes. The next game, I was a starter on varsity. This revelation of inner strength showed others and me that I had something deep inside which I could connect with and release. This same spirit source would allow me to excel in writing and in my playing music alone or in a group.

My love of music came natural and has been sustaining, but I had to learn the skills of playing. I would practice my cornet during "Band," the last period at school each day, but also I took my cornet home on the weekends to play alone in my bedroom sitting by the window facing the town and the mill. Here I would run the scales searching for a clarity and tone. Mom loved it when I finally got off scales and began playing "real songs." Soon I began buying sheet music and sought a certain vibrato of tone that I showered upon the town from my window. At times I would be excused from school to ride in a hearse to proudly play "Taps" at some veteran's grave site. At football games and concerts Mom and Dad would show up to cheer. Inside the band itself I learned how to work as part of a group, and though there was always some rivalry between the brass and the woodwinds sections, we worked as a unit on or off the field.

The band also proved to be a great place for making friends and meeting girls. When the first school dance rolled around, a Saddie Hawkins girl's choice, I was relieved to be asked by Janet, a fellow trumpeter. Back then we still dressed up for dances, and so I showed up for this first "date" in a charcoal suit, skinny black tie, and black spade shoes which I'd worked into a spit shine. Janet was tall and thin, but had a great sense of humor. We joked with each other and at others. However, that night the joke was on me as she in her pretty tunic dress danced right out of my arms and began playing the room, flirting with every guy there. I stood around at the punch table or leaned against the wall watching her. My ego was hurt, and any fantasy of being on a date was crushed. In fact later that evening I fell back into my old pattern of not taking the girl back to her door. I dropped old Janet off at the foot of her stairs. When our driver brother David watched this, he just shook his head. "I get you," he said, "but man, you still have to be a gentleman." The next day, I knew he was right; I'd let my hurt ego turn into anger and resentment, a fault which I would carry much of my life. Unfortunate as this was, that date had broken the ice with my being with a high school girl.

By far my best relationship in the band was with Annie, a pretty senior girl who for whatever reason took a liking to me. As I moved up from third to second to first trumpet chair beside her, we began to share more and more. Our easy rapport could also be heard in our horns which would lead to our playing a duet in the regional contest. We both felt a kinship and were happy with just talk. She would actually listen and sweetly smile, her deep blue eyes open and accepting, helping me to get over my hurdles of dealing with both school and girls. Of course, I developed a big crush on her, which proved awkward when Ted her senior boyfriend got word of it.

One day between classes, Ted bumped into me, and brushed me back against the wall. "Hey, bud, you know who I am?" I nodded. "And I guess you know that Annie is my girl." Again I nodded yes, and so he backed off, "So stay cool about it," his finger pressed against my chest. "You get me?" I stood staring in stillness, my fondness for Annie tucked deep into my pocket. While we guys were being emotional about it, Annie had it all in control. Her love was for him, but her caring extended to me and to others. Like Joy, who would come over after school to teach me to dance in our kitchen, she was my girl-friend, not girlfriend, and they both helped me be more comfortable with girls and myself. Lying in bed staring up at the crack in the ceiling I began to see how some people come into our lives as a challenge, some as a pure blessing, and we can learn from both. The band had brought me Janet, but it also brought me Annie and Joy.

However, it was in Miss Monaco's fourth period English class that I first fell in love. Not with her, dressed like a nun without the head gear, in long black skirt and carrying a wooden pointer which she could whack on the desk for attention. The true dictator of language and discipline, she taught language arts with a drill sergeant's sternness. We filled our notebooks with the usage rules scrawled on the board and recited them upon command. She quickly knew all of our names and could call us out on demand when it was our turn to recite rules or memorized poems. And yet over the decades after graduating, again and again I would hear her praised for how she helped us rise above our street talk. "Man, I hated and feared her," they would say shaking their head and adding, "But she sure taught me what I needed to know."

No, it was not Miss Monaco that I loved, but Barbara who sat across the room from me so often raising her hand to answer. I'll admit that I first fell for her clear Polish-Irish face and the bobbing of her strawberry blond pony tail. She, like about a third of the other kids from town, had gone to the Catholic grade school, whereas I was a "public," and so she was a fresh and lovely face and had spirit. It took weeks before I approached her after class with some made up question about English gerunds or participles. Turns out, we were both taken with each other, I with slim good looks, and she with a sunny outlook and sweet smile. And so, we began meeting on the steps outside of school to talk, or I would quietly walk her up the hill to her St. Agnes Church after school.

I knew that I was crossing some social and religious lines by dating a Catholic girl, but by the late 1950s this had come to be seen as an accepted risk—as long as it didn't go too far and become an inter-religious marriage. As a young Protestant I had heard from the pulpit warnings about the gambling practices of the Catholics who sponsored bingo games in the church basement, drank actual wine in church, and who worshiped a Pope in Rome. Barbara admitted that she had been warned about the shallow faith of the Protestants who denied both the Pope and Mary their proper place. My friend Joy had once been told by a priest not to attend our youth group meetings or parties for fear of corruption. Our religions would clearly have us separated and praying for each other's lost souls. And yet, Barbara and I found ourselves in that great place where change comes on. Love and marriage were breaking the ethnic boundaries as well as this Catholic and Protestant split. As teenagers, Barbara and I just listened to our hearts.

That year, 1957, a high school rock group from Mingo had a hit song. The Savoys was made up of four doo-wop singers joined by older crooner Joey Farr. He and this group renamed The Mingo Men recorded the sweet ballad "Devotion," which suggests our whole image of dating and love back then. Within two weeks of Barbara and I meeting after school and at school events, we were deemed to be "going steady." Today's youth often meet in packs of mixed boys and girls out for fun together, and without the immediate assumption of their being coupled off. Back then, if you were seen together more than twice, it was a given that you were "with" them or "going steady together." And so we were, then and for six more years when we ultimately saw ourselves as separate persons, but that story lies around the long corner.

Music played a large part in my youth as crooners and ballad singers gave way to rock-n-rollers. Again, thanks to brother David, I was allowed to sit and listen with his friends as they spun 45 records in someone's bedroom or rec-room. We followed the local groups thinking this was another way, besides sports, to reach fame and glory. Local guitar rocker Woodie Yingst was playing with Buddy Sharp and the Shakers on their hit, "Linda Lee," and George Otis was singing with the Stereos, a black R&B group with the hit song "I Really Love You." While Elvis was knocking out rock-a-billy songs like "It's Alright,' and "Blue Suede Shoes," brother David led me to harder rock songs on Pittsburgh's radical radio stations WEEP and WHOD (WAMO). Here through DJs Porkey Chedwick and Mary Dee we first heard racially diverse rhythm and blues rock from such artists as Little Richard, Chuck Berry, Bo Diddley, and we could even hear Gene Vincent's banned "Woman Love" for the first time. I began to see music as a way of expressing uncovered tensions and deep urges long before I saw writing in this way.

On February 4, 1959, I watched my brother sit and cry on the stairs. It was "the day the music died," when his hero Buddy Holly perished in a small plane crash, along with singers Ritchie Valens and the Big Bopper. We had rocked and bopped with Buddy Holly and the Crickets for several years of hit tunes like "Peggy Sue," "Maybe Baby," "I'm Looking for Someone to Love," and "Raining in My Heart." We had each held a girl close while dancing to Valens' haunting "Oh Donna." We felt that we "owned" their music as our own story. Rock music was our anthem, and as teenagers it spoke our emotions and gave us a culture and freedom.

And so, it was no surprise that I begged and saved for a guitar of my own. The first one came from my truck driving Uncle Ray who bought or won it in a bar on his truck route. It was an old acoustic with slightly warped neck and worn metal strings, but I banged away chords on it till my fingers stung and ached, and finally calloused over, like my teenage emotions. And then, on my 16th birthday my father surprised me with a black and white Stratotone electric guitar bought from Sears Roebuck for $50 ($400 today). Tears came to my eyes just looking at its cool cutaway body, such a straight neck, such curves, sweeter than any girl's. And then Dad brought up from the basement the amplifier which he and his tv repairman buddy had made. Though heavy with tubes, oak frame, upholstered front, and with a loose jack plug, I viewed it as a sign of Dad's love even as I lugged it up and down stairs.

Forced by my noise (right word for it) to find a practice space in the basement, I would sit and listen to records over and over, then strain to hear and play the right chords. Doc Watson's and Mel Bay's guitar books led me from "Down in the Valley" and "My Darling Clementine" to playing Johnny Cash's "Walk the Line" and Elvis' "Hound Dog." But, except for family and friends Kenny and Billy, I was a basement guitar player. That was until band camp that summer of 1960 when I met up with drummer Joey and guitarist Rich. We began to practice together in my basement or at Tony's barbershop after hours. Rough at first, we started to get into a groove and built up a repertoire of three whole songs. Another guitarist was drafted, mostly for his fine Les Paul guitar which Rich quickly adopted and played.

Our first gig was at a youth barn dance for the Richmond Grange Hall. Expecting that they would have a record player and that we would be the feature with our three live tunes, we were shocked to learn that we were it—the "Band," expected to play the whole night, and those young kids really wanted to dance, dance, dance. That night we did our three tunes twice and then we became true musicians and launched into songs we had never played or ones we just made up. Rich created a version of "The Twist" and the kids started drilling their toes into the old wooden floor boards. We were truly with it and sharing it with others. Later, with our excitement high from a performance, we divided up the twelve dollars between the four of us and drove home in my family station wagon, stopping for milk shakes and sundaes at the local Dairy-Q.

Though we had dared to sing a few songs at our last gig, we knew that we were musicians and not singers. So, when a rival doo-wop group asked us to join with them, we took the offer seriously. We began practicing together and had our simple three chord songs down pat. In that group were classmates Pete, Donny, Guy, Johnny, and Noony— nine of us in all. We practiced at Tony's barbershop a couple times, then one fateful Saturday afternoon, we gathered at Pete's place where the Ferroni family lived a block away from my own house. We stood on the front porch, knocked, and the most lovely young woman came to the door. With short dark hair, smiling eyes, and snug fitting slacks, this maiden opened the door and my heart. This was Ann, my future wife, though none of us dreamed it then. Well, maybe I did, many times, though I was still going steady with Barbara. I think I just said to myself, "If ever..."

When the Mingo Community Center had their next youth dance at the city building, we pleaded and were finally invited to play. That meant a trip down to Weisberger's clothing store where we astounded the clerk with a request for nine matching maroon shirts. She brought out Freddie Weisberger who grinned as he questioned us, "Are you guys for real? This is a special order you know. There's no going back." When we handed him the hard earned cash from our yard cutting, theater ushering, baby sitting, even bottle returning, he began writing up the order. We were serious musicians, and back then you helped convince yourself and the audience of this by the way you dressed.

The night we played, we set up the amps, guitars, and drum set, then adjourned to the back alley parking lot where a row of cars were parked along with the town's police cruiser. Several of the guys had lit up to "calm their nerves." I was just breathing it all in: the roar of the mill, the glare of the street light on the cars, the faces of my friends. Barbara and others were inside waiting to dig or disdain our playing. We knew the scene because we'd been part of it for years. There was some talk among the guys, mostly boasting about how we would kill them tonight. Some long silences and suddenly Mrs. Hoff appeared at the back door, "Okay, boys, it's time for you to go on."

As planned, we entered the arena like cool gladiators. Our original band group opened with our instrumental, "Girl in the Red Dress." People nodded, clapped some, and then our doo-wop singers emerged from the back door amidst applause. Rich played a couple notes for the singers to key to, and then we were off, instruments following and answering each other, singers listening and taking it to another level. No music sheets, all of it coming from somewhere inside. And the crowd loved it almost as much as we did bringing it on. *There is nothing like this,* I said to myself and then out loud to the band. Pete looked at Guy and Guy at me, looking at Rich. We all felt it and nodded so. Four songs, and we were off. Like that, the gig was over, only it would go on in our heads for weeks till graduation came and we split for summer jobs and college. The group would never play again.

*   *   *

Before I graduated, a couple key events happened. First was the day that Jane, the school secretary, came into our homeroom and asked for my best friend Kenny and me to follow her down to the principal's office. "What have we done?" I whispered to Kenny, who shrugged. When we got there, Shirley Mae was seated on the office bench. I knew she couldn't do anything wrong, but she too shrugged her shoulders and looked into our eyes. Finally we were taken in to Principal Muth's office.

"Please sit," he said. "And don't worry, it's nothing bad. I have something to share with you."

We all breathed that sigh of relief, though suspense was still thick in the air.

"I'm happy to report that we have tabulated the points for class rank and you three are at the top."

Now the smiles came. Was that all?

"And though the scores were very close, even decimal points apart, I can tell you that Larry here is your class valedictorian."

What? screamed in my head. Though a high achiever, I had always figured that Kenny or Shirley would be the chosen one.

"Excuse me for asking," Kenny said. "What is the score based upon?"

"No, that's fine. We follow a detailed list for grade average and club activities."

There was a pause. "And though Shirley had the highest academic standing, you and Larry had far more extracurricular activities."

What we all knew and nobody spoke was that to help out her family Shirley had been steered into a business program and had to clerk after school. There were no points for that and no way she could keep up with work and do the clubs.

Finally, Principal Muth shook all of our hands and said our parents and the school were very proud of us. I don't remember leaving the office, but I recall a moment out in the hall where I actually hugged Shirley and whispered, "You deserve this, not me."

She smiled back and gave me a small kiss on the cheek, whispering, "I'm happy for you," then disappeared down the hallway.

As valedictorian I was given the big responsibility of delivering the commencement address. I had already won the American Legion essay contest writing on the theme "What Democracy Means to Me," and I had penned the class poem and song. With the English teacher's approval and edits, my speech was approved. I recall little of that exciting night except the faces of my classmates in their graduation garb and the few minutes of my speech. It was the Kennedy era, and we were becoming involved in the war in Vietnam. John Fitzgerald Kennedy and his beautiful wife Jacqueline were our new ideals, if not idols. So it was only natural for me to borrow the words and intention from his inaugural address. At the old auditorium we filed into our front rows. The lights were brought up, and after a few welcome speeches, I was brought on stage. I looked out at my family, girlfriend, and classmates. Following thank yous to teachers, coaches, and families, I spoke from the heart, concluding with this line from Kennedy: "As we go out into the world, let us all remember these words of our fine president, 'Ask not what your country can do for you, but what you can do for your country,'" and was greeted with much applause. In the next hour, we each had been handed our diploma as though it were a ticket to somewhere great. Then we marched down the aisle and out the doors onto the street.

Chapter Four: College & Life Lessons

That summer of 1961 I worked as a playground teacher outside of the Harmony Elementary School in Mingo. My father's friend Don, on the Park and Recreation Board, moved my name along. When the director Margaret Ross hired me on, she looked me over, shook her head and asked, "Are you sure you want to do this, fellow? You're the first man we've hired—ever."

I smiled, "Yes, I do." I had read a book on teaching that year which strongly suggested that if you hadn't worked with children by the time you entered college, you probably weren't meant to be a teacher. And so I deliberately tested myself to see who I was and what I might be meant to do.

Soon I got to know the kids of George's Run by pushing them on swings, patching their wounds with Band-Aids, and playing checkers with them. I learned that to be their friend and also maintain some order I would have to balance my distance with them. Eventually I taught many of them to play chess and to gather for the bookmobile and read together on the school steps. I broke up fights and contained bullies, conducted a pet show and a penny carnival. I even organized a junior track meet in the grassy field, complete with prize ribbons that I and Barbara had made. As the children and I worked together, we became friends, each of us learning from each other the secret of being a good teacher. Though the pay was low at a dollar an hour, I passed this first test of working well with children, yet I still had much to learn about teaching.

Without any help from my high school, I had applied to two colleges: Miami University of Ohio (a state school) and Muskingum College (a Presbyterian liberal arts school), and I was also offered the valedictorian's scholarship to nearby Steubenville College. In this working-class town with 66 in my graduating class that 1961, I was not surprised to be among the only six who went on to higher education. The rest took good jobs in the steel mills or on the railroads, married and raised children, or enlisted or were drafted into military services, many in the succeeding years to fight and die in the war in Vietnam.

My brother David was then a sophomore at Marysville College, a small Presbyterian school in Tennessee where he was considering the ministry. We were the first Smiths to enter college, something my father wanted and perhaps dreamed of for himself, so much so that he took out a second mortgage, despite my mother's concern. Married for 20 years by then, she had seen the money come and go, and yet their old house had not changed despite Dad's promises. Once in the kitchen near tears after dinner, she had pleaded, "When am I ever going to get my new house?" No one really had an answer for that.

Nestled in the rolling hills of central Ohio, Muskingum College had a population to match the 1,400 population of the town, New Concord. I liked its smallness and that it was only two hours away from home. That first Sunday after church, my father and mother helped me pack up my list of "Things to Bring to College," including a much loved trench coat and a black umbrella, two things I never would be seen with in Mingo. On Barbara's back porch steps the night before, we had kissed goodbye with tears welling in our eyes and a promise to write each day, which I kept (perhaps my best training in writing). Though Dad and I had visited the campus once, it seemed as though I were going to a foreign land, and in many ways I was—a kid from a working-class small town entering a cultured liberal arts college. Excitement and fear mixed and yielded uncertainty. And so it was a long, quiet drive, with me sitting in the back seat and no one more anxious than I. Though a valedictorian with a small scholarship, I truly feared flunking out and disappointing my family, most of all, my father. In some real ways I saw myself as carrying a banner for my family and town and a way of life. During the four years I was there, this feeling only developed.

After unloading my belongings in a dorm room which seemed like a walk-in closet, my mother made my bed. She joked, "Well, son, this is the last time I'll be doing this," adding an "I hope" which struck me. My roommate hadn't arrived, as we were early in the day, and there was no one to welcome us, so we gawked through the windows of the cafeteria then got back into the car and drove through campus—old brick buildings, a football field and stands, a large pond with a couple swans, more brick buildings—and then we were out the front gate. Sensing their unease, I offered, "You can take me back to the dorm if you'd like."

Dad countered, "How about we first get us a piece of pie and some coffee?" In the town's only diner, beside the only gas station, at the only traffic light, we stopped. Inside, a friendly hostess showed us to a booth, and with coffee our talk became more easy. As I sat across from my parents, I watched their faces and could almost taste the sacrifice they had made for me, seasoned with their hopes. I know that they never felt at home at the college, and in some ways neither did I. For those four years I struggled to reconcile my two worlds at what some have called, "this fine place so far from home."

I must add that I did love the learning, the culture of ideas, the movies, concerts, and guest speakers. I attended all of those offerings. In the classroom I found a real excitement in discovering new thoughts, seeing deeper and wider connections, working things out live in the classroom and talking them over in the dorm rooms. Some of my professors were extraordinary persons as well as teachers. The art teacher invited us into his home in small groups where we drank coffee and talked about art and life. Some professors were rather provincial and also ministers tied to the Presbyterian Church. Most of the students seemed bound for careers in teaching or the ministry. As someone who had attended the Catholic Mass with my girlfriend, I knew enough to pity any student who was not Protestant. Twice a week we had to show up for "chapel" sessions at Brown Chapel where attendance was taken by upper-class students, and a sermon was the typical program. I was struck on hearing the student body president declare, "Muskingum is a small Christian college ...for small Christians." Was that a praise or a warning?

As "frosh" we did have to endure the slights of upperclassmen and even the awkwardness of forced social events like the faculty tea. Here every freshman had to move along a greeting line and meet each faculty member who seemed equally ill at ease. The dorms were separated by physical valleys and hills into men's and women's. In fair weather we were socialized by half of us men reluctantly trudging over to the girl's dorms to sit and eat in mixed company. Actually I rather liked this. Women held wider conversations, including the arts and society. Heaven help you though if you were seated with an upperclassman with a serious research topic. During that first month, we freshmen attended church and Sunday School, until we gradually realized that neither was required. In a much larger vision we began asking serious questions of our religion and faith, finding our own path.

As time went on, however, what I missed most at Muskingum was any recognition of my social background. Here we were in the foothills of Appalachia, yet no mention was made of its land and culture. And the term "working-class" seemed reserved for political science majors. This assumed rightness of the middle to upper class life and culture was spread before us, and we were to model and pull ourselves up to it. With my firm roots in family, place, and equality, this ignorance seemed a wrong, if not a crime. While I was struggling to work out the relationship of my background with college life, the school seemed to do so by denying the former. What did they know of storytelling, equanimity, looking out for each other, making do and getting by? Inside I carried a sense of violation even while I sought to succeed at the school's academics. Fortunately my study of literature helped, if not saved me. I read rebel authors like Henry David Thoreau or writers aware of social class like John Steinbeck and William Faulkner, and quietly I resisted the school's emphasis on social status and sameness, ironically assumed from a cultural ignorance. I remember one night talking to my roommate Pat, "I mean, Jesus Christ himself was a working-class person who remained loyal to his small town of Nazareth." He stood there nodding as I went on, "Look how he denied inequality by washing the feet of others, and he spoke for the poor ….'Blessed are the poor.' Why can't they see that empathy and acceptance are central to Christianity?" He shrugged his shoulders and climbed into bed.

The writing done at college was chiefly expository essay writing, making a thesis point and backing it up, and so I gained some skills in precision, reasoning, and proving a point. My study of literature urged me on to writing poems shared at first only in letters to Barbara but stored in a black notebook. The college may have denied my culture, but it was giving me the skills to write of it.

At least once a month I would hitchhike home from New Concord on old Route 40, the National Road. I and several others would be standing out at the edge of town with a sign—"Home to Steubenville" or wherever—posted onto our bag. Typically I would keep walking slowly with my thumb out and eventually be picked up by a salesman or semi-truck driver willing to break the rules for some shared company. Never did that imagined convertible full of pretty women pull over for me. Mostly it was me and the driver sharing some talk to quiet our loneliness. Often I listened while staring out the window longing to be home with my sweetheart and family. After a month of college I desperately needed to just be myself at home.

Though hitchhiking was more common then, a few times I would only make it partway home. One day sticks with me for a couple of reasons. Early in the day I had been treated well by a young philosophy professor, Dr. Elkins, who changed his schedule to allow me to take an early exam so I could get on the road to home. He understood and accepted this. At one point he came over to say, "Larry, I'm going over to the rec center for some coffee. Can I bring something back for you—a sandwich or muffin, a coffee?" Never had I been treated so nicely by a professor, in or out of a classroom.

Later that day I found myself stranded in Bridgeport, Ohio, across the river from Wheeling and the last 20 miles from home. A chilling wind was blowing, and traffic was rushing past me, and so, cold and getting a little desperate, I stepped into a local diner. The warmth inside swept over me as I took a seat at the counter. When the tall blonde waitress came over, I asked for just a cup of coffee. Millie was the name on her uniform, and so I said, "Oh, thank you, Millie." She laughed and told me, "Funny thing, hon, I'm really just a Janet in a Millie uniform." She had this pretty smile watching me drink, then she pointed me to the restroom. When I came back, there was my coffee refilled along with a big slice of apple pie. "Hey," she said, "I got a daughter down at Ohio University. I know what it's like. This is on me." With only us two at the counter, we talked. Then she allowed me to use the house phone to call my father (her idea) to come and pick me up. God, I missed good people like this. I felt already at home.

When Dad arrived in the Chevy, I was waiting on the corner. He called, "Hey, jump in." I did and we swung around in a parking lot and headed back up north on old Route 7 that ran past our house. Dad had this funny smirk on his face.

"What's up?" I asked. "Something funny?"

He looked over at me. "Heck, you're old enough to know this stuff."

"What...What stuff?"

"Well, Bridgeport is known by some for two things, its bridges...and its houses of prostitution." I stared over at him. "You've heard by now the Biblical meaning of to know someone, I guess?" I nodded. "Well, son, you see that bar, the Four Leaf Clover, right next to the diner...well, let's just say, it's girls are known by many."

Thrown back by this talk from my church-going father, I just laughed and didn't dare ask how he came to know all of this. He was a railroader after all. On the rest of the drive home I told him the stories of the kindness of the professor and the waitress. His response was one sentence, "It's not the place that matters, son; it's the people."

At home they had saved a dinner for me, and I sat with Mom and ate her bean soup and corn bread. She asked about my classes, and I told her I was switching from math to English. I had taken Calculus I at 8 a.m., and sat in the abstract air of it all till I desperately wanted to escape. In freshman English we wrote about the great literature we were reading, and I felt myself grounded in the stories of people's lives again. "What will you do with it?" Mom asked, and I shrugged, "Teach, I suppose." She was fine with that. I didn't risk saying become a writer, though she would have approved. It was she after all who handed me a copy of *The Catcher in the Rye* while I was a high school freshman; she who would call my brother and I down late at night to watch the Smothers Brothers on Jack Parr's *Tonight Show*, she who was moved to tears over television drama.

My next move was to jump in the car and head up to Barbara's house. She was living at home while going to Steubenville College to become—what else, a teacher. After some wild kissing in the car, we would drive to a Big Boys restaurant to sip coffee and talk. I was glad she was doing well, and my switch to English as a major pleased her. "I just knew you weren't a math and science guy." Then back at her house we would hold each other quietly on the couch until she or I couldn't stay awake. Life was no longer a destiny, but lived around me. On Sunday we would have a sad parting, then Mom and Dad would drive a gloomy guy back to a campus he liked but struggled to accept, a place that didn't accept him or his world.

*   *   *

The summer of 1962 I worked the kitchen of the mezzanine restaurant in the Hub Department Store in Steubenville. For years I didn't know it or the mezzanine existed, dining instead on the counter stools of Woolworth's Five and Dime where you could get a hot dog and a root beer for a quarter. But this year I moved up to local elegance at my mother's favorite place to dine when shopping. So impressed was she that I would be working there in my all-white uniform that she told her friends I was a cook. Really I was the person dishing out cooked food at the hot table, but it all came to matter.

The dining room was run by two sisters: Beatrice as the big cook and boss, Bertha as the elegant hostess in charge of the waitress staff who all dressed in black skirts and neat white blouses with a red cloth carnation pinned at the breast pocket. No slave driver, Bertha led by modeling and she looked like one, training the "girls" to speak with patience and grace to everyone their side of the serving counter, including the older ladies running the big dish washer and scrubbing pots and pans in back. Everyone was to receive a meal a day, though choices were few—usually macaroni and cheese served with stewed tomatoes, the soup of the day, or a burger from the grill with fries. I also did the fries.

Dolly fried those burgers and everything else that came from the grill. She was a tall, strong black woman who moved in a slow dance, never rushing but always delivering on time. Dolly would whisper advice to guide me, always calling me "Honey." Beside her was Tommy, Bertha's nephew, running the soda fountain, and on the side, Shirley. She was the opposite of Dolly, efficient but jumpy and small enough to take the abuse of head cook Beatrice, who would pass by and find some fault. "Clean up that counter! Why are you all just standing around?"

This was the first thing I learned, "Larry, never just stand around. Always keep busy. Use that cloth to clean up the steam table, blanche some more fries, do some set-ups." This came from Darlene, my boss and trainer. Ten years older, Darlene was a real woman and a "fox" to me at nineteen and old enough to dream of her. Trim and quick without rushing, she managed to look good in her white uniform—mine covered in spaghetti sauce or whatever else I was serving. Working so close I sensed her every body movement, and came to coordinate with her animation in a kind of smooth jitterbug. Once I wore cologne to work to impress her, but she just smiled and said softly, "Hey, don't waste your good money on that stuff," adding, "When working the table, you'll always end up smelling like the food."

Darlene taught me efficiency and focus which marked her work, and I tried to adopt it as my own. Sure we were just placing food on a plate, but it was done with finesse, keeping the foods neatly separate and setting that bit of dark green endive just so on that white plate. We gave each plate a kind of dignity that made everything look and taste better.

The third thing I learned was pacing—Dolly gave me that. "Honey, just keep moving. You'll get there when it's time. Rush it," and here she looked over at Tommy who'd spun a chocolate milk shake onto the floor that morning, "and you'll make a mess for all us to clean up." The next year, I would be working in the steel mill, when an older worker stopped us college boys with, "Hey, you guys, we don't sweat in here. Get me?"

By the end of the summer Darlene's sister Marie came in to work the table with me, but she couldn't get it. "Rush it, and ruin it," I finally told her, "One thing at a time," but she didn't listen and the waitresses started sending back the plates, "I can't serve this," they'd say snearing from Marie to me, and I'd gently take over. "Always look at your plate," I'd say. I was being Darlene and Marie was I.

I learned a lot about food and work that summer, more than I would in the steel mill where the models weren't as good. The work you do does matter, and not so much what that work is as how you do it, and who the people are that you work with. Each job can teach you something. Though I left that summer, I still imagine all those folks working well together there.

*   *   *

In retrospect I see that a major epiphany about college and life came during my junior year. Like most college students, I had come to question most, if not all, things established: social mores and customs, education, institutions, religion, even my faith in the future. These deep questionings, often ignored in classrooms, were shared in late night dorm room discussions, and often recorded in my daily journaling and in the letters written home to girlfriend Barbara. I was coming through this educational system to some sense of my self as a whole person. In a course on American Romanticism for example, I found fellow questioners through the writings of Ralph Waldo Emerson, Henry David Thoreau, and Emily Dickinson. From them I gathered the concept of *ambivalence*—"the presence of two opposing ideas, attitudes, or emotions at the same time; a feeling of uncertainty about something due to mental conflict" (*North America Dictionary*). Its brother, ambiguity, came along with it, allowing doubt to open the door to uncertainty and to mystery. I had come to see that education was not a matter of having the right answers but asking the right questions and living without certainty. Hearing this inquiry voiced and demonstrated in their literature had a profound effect on me, offering both recognition and inspiration. Life was now fluid for me, and writing was capable of both revelation and service.

I saw how my personal struggles at college had risen from having one foot on the college campus, the other on the streets of home. How common and legitimate were these mixed feelings of longing and of not belonging! I both loved and hated both worlds—the insights and the lies of college education (giving them what they wanted on exams), the comfort and the apathy of home life (greeting friends then just sitting with them in bars); mixed in me were the practical worlds of tools and the abstract methods of reasoning. These dual views living inside of me deserved this same ongoing questioning. Like most college students I developed a sharpened sense of judgment and sarcasm, falling asleep in a required course on the Bible, yet answering back on exams with what they expected to hear. In a course entitled "Modern Christian Thought" I heard a theology professor mocking the Catholic faith in Mary as divine. When I dared to raise my hand and ask, "Well, if you can believe that Christ rose from the dead, why can't you believe that Mary also ascended?" A hush fell in the room, as he turned on me and asked, "Well, young man, you have a brain don't you, you can reason can't you?" That night, when I reported all this to Barbara on the phone, her only response was a gasp and "Oh, Larry, please be careful."

I began to look around for signs of rebellion on our quiet campus. When John Glenn, a New Concord native and Muskingum grad, orbited in space, the campus became invaded by the state and national media. Their trucks and reporters were everywhere. At one point an interviewer asked an outspoken senior what he thought of it all, and he bluntly told them "John Glenn is being sold to the American public like a bar of soap." This was reported in *Esquire* magazine. When another senior, later a friend and fellow writer, David Budbill published a sexual story in the college literary magazine, *The Angry I*, he was promptly expelled.

To my surprise and joy faculty members rallied and had him reinstated. Among most of the campus he became a martyr and hero. Also, at one point a married couple had invited another couple to their off-campus home. When it was discovered that wine had been consumed, a Presbyterian campus taboo, they too were threatened with expulsion. If the Beat writers and others were leading a wild rebellion elsewhere, Muskingum was maintaining its conservative *loco parentis* status well. This wall of resistance I came to feel deserved questioning and attack.

I had come to see that real learning existed beyond the classroom in my deep readings and my journaling of these areas of ambiguity and ambivalence. I'm afraid Barbara was the recipient of much of this doubt spreading. Equally comforting and troubling, this questioning of all became challenging and led to a solitary path as my way toward understanding self and life. Its culmination arrived with the final breakup of Larry and Barbara after six years. It's a scene I will never forget:

I am a junior home for Christmas vacation, and when I call up Barbara, she says she wants to come right over. "Sure," I say. "I can't wait to see you." Minutes later she pulls up and standing at the front door balks at coming inside. I read a new sternness in her face and eyes. "What's up?" I ask.

She shakes her head and speaks, "Okay, can we step into your hallway?" There in the dim light and silence she holds out her hand. In it are my high school ring and the jeweled fraternity pin used to pledge our soft engagement to marry.

In a gasp, it comes out, "Larry, it's over."

"What...what's over?"

"All of it. We're over." *Pause, take a breath.*

"We both know that we are through," she says while staring into my wounded face and pulling back her hand. "You're a good guy really, but I just don't love you anymore, and I don't feel you love me."

I can't breathe. "But..." is all I manage.

And she, "I don't want or need to do this anymore."

Whatever words I might use never get a chance, because she turns just that quick and goes out the door. Or maybe it just seemed that quick as I stand there in mute shock. My whole world has just come crashing down on me. As I watch her pull away, I wave, absurdly thinking the words *Merry Christmas*, then I rush up the stairs to the empty solace of my room and bed.

It would take months for any light to enter. That whole December I moped around the house listening to the sad, sweet trumpet music of Al Hirt's "I Can't Get Started," and I truly couldn't—get started. My lying on the couch near the Christmas tree felt more like living with a cross. Eventually my sisters Janis and Debbie would cry out, "Mom, he's playing that song again." Phone calls, letters, even my showing up outside of Barbara's college classroom did no good. She was doing what I didn't have the courage to do or admit to.

On New Year's Eve I went out with my good friends Joy and Kenny to a bar in Weirton. The place was bright and full of people I didn't know. We had a couple beers, then while dancing close to a slow song with Joy, she stopped me right there on the dance floor. "Hon, listen, I love you like a brother, you know that, and I always will. But you're holding me like I'm Barbara, and I'm not." She kissed me on the cheek and went back to the bar. She was right. And back at the bar then on the drive home I apologized probably too many times. Clearly this grieving over losing Barbara and my whole life plan was the darkest I had ever been. I had lost innocence and myself. That next week I had to be convinced by Dad that I must go back to college. "This moping, son, it's no good for you or anyone." He waited for me to look up. "You're punishing yourself and those that do love you." His words struck like a bell. Loss had shrunken my world, but suffering had opened my heart.

When I returned home for spring break, I had something to do. First, I called Barbara, and when I heard her voice, I said, "Barbara, listen please. I need you to know something. This has all been hard, and I want you to know that I love you, but I'm not in love with you anymore." Long pause, then she said, "Good," and we both just hung up. The next morning I went down into the back yard, and I built a big fire in a wash tub. Standing before it I burned all of our love letters, even old photos of us together. It got to be a pretty big blaze, as I stood around poking it. The hurt and anger were turning to ash. Finally Mom came down from the house to ask, "Honey, are you okay?"

"Yes," I told her. "This is the best I've felt in a long, long time." I was absurdly happy and could breathe again. I didn't explain, but my gut told me that I needed to really let go and accept that life was not a clear pattern or path to follow, but a spiral, with ups and downs, opening to possibility. Life did not go "Good, better, best," as our civics teacher had sung to us, adding "Never let it rest, till your good is better, and your better best." It just doesn't really go that way, and standing before the slow burning fire I understood and felt that. I was more in tune with Thomas Moore, who sees the movement of loving as necessary. He wisely declares, "Love is a means of entry and our guide.

Love keeps us on the labyrinthine path." Just as I recognized love as imperfect, I also knew that I was not my brother David, that math was not my gift, that colleges could be biased, and that my life was not over. Thank God for choice. It was still possible to heal and grow. I could embrace the loose, irrational, even absurd nature of life. Staring into the fire, I knew that I could rise from these ashes.

*   *   *

That summer I would be tested by fire in so many ways, including the literal fires of the blast furnaces of Weirton Steel. The mills were hiring the sons and daughters of their millworkers. And so I drove over to the West Virginia plant, filled out the application form and waited, and I waited. Finally my truck driving Uncle Ray said, "Son, you have to show them that you really want the job. Call them or better yet, go over to their offices again." He was absolutely right, and after several calls, I was told to come in for work.

The steel mill and the city of Weirton are one. The main street runs right through the mill...tin plant buildings and smoking blast furnaces on the left, to the right the rolling and processing plants. Smoke and ore dust falling over everything. I had driven through many times, only now I was coming to earn, not a living, but the money to pay for my college education. My wage jumped five times from the dollar an hour I earned working at the playground or as the short order cook at the Hub department store.

Before I could be hired, I was given a physical exam that I won't forget. It played out like a film scene. While seated on an examination table in a hospital robe, I hear through the curtains as an older mill worker is being told. "I'm sorry to tell you this, but you have lung disease." Silence, then he asks. "Well, what does this mean, doc?"

And the doctor says, "Black lung...you have black lung and can't work any longer, here or maybe anywhere." Another long, long silence and suddenly the doctor walks through that curtain to me at 20 sitting there in my hospital robe about to be born into labor. Having passed the exam, I was instructed to buy good steel toed boots and to wear long sleeved working shirts. Then I was handed an orange-brown safety hat. I would work on the labor gang around the blast furnaces, the same area where my father was working as a brakeman.

We drove to work together that summer, Dad dropping me off at the mill gate. I was happy to work with him, though later he would confess his misgiving about having me work near him. Driving home he explained, "I didn't know what you'd think, seeing how simple and hard my work is." How strange that my view was the opposite, witnessing the skills and sacrifice he had made all those years. It's true that some railroaders are pretty rowdy. One train crew waved a gallon jug of beer from the engine to us college boys on the labor gang. Dad never did that, nor did he bring the mill home with him as some men did. He would transition on the drive home and emerge from the basement clean and ready to be with family. While driving home, I was thinking of my father's long years working in the mill and wondering at the hidden cost of this job.

It was hard sweaty work, and much standing around. At first, when we finished a job we would seek out Bob our foreman to tell him we were through. Finally he told us, "You go back to where your job is, and I'll find you. You get it?" His job was finding us work, and we were making that hard for him. From older workers, we learned how to pace the work, not rush it. And like being a freshman at college, the first weeks were a test to see if we really wanted the job. Early on, Bob sent me down the slag alley to the pig iron machine. It meant walking down a narrow lane with buildings on one side, the hot slag being poured off the other side into train ladles, hot sparks flying everywhere. Facing it was not a dare, but a rite of passage. I stood looking down the alley until one older guy came up and, over the roar of the blast furnace, shouted, "You can do it, kid. Move right along, and if them sparks land on you, just brush 'em off with your gloves." And I did it then and again till the risk became common, as did watching each job for danger and working around it. The rest of that rainy day I used a long metal poker and knocked out the heavy pigs that got stuck in the pig iron belt circulating above my head. After showering in that big stall with the older men, I dressed and headed up to punch out. Dad was already waiting across the street to drive home. When he asked me how the day went, I just smiled and said, "Good. It went well. When do I get paid?"

*   *   *

That transition summer of 1964, I went through a series of blind dates, most of them set up, much to my mother's chagrin, by her friend Wanda. I'll confess the first two girls were "easy," offering themselves to me on the first date, not because I was such a great catch but because both had a low self-image. We talked instead, and though all were hungry for loving, we parted. Then a neighbor girl, Francis, hooked me up with her young friend from Ursuline College. She was sweet, smart, and thinking of becoming a nun. We dated twice, had great talks, but she was only 17, and though things sparked between us, the fire just wasn't there. I'd been through mistaking a friend as a girlfriend, and so we too parted.

I was almost convinced I would never love someone again when Francis' sister Cecilia set up a date with her nursing school roommate. It was Ann, the young woman I had met years ago when our rock group practiced at her Grandma's house. It was to be a double date with Ann and me to play tennis with Cecilia and her fiancé Albert at the city's court. But then Ann refused because she'd been burned on blind dates arranged by friends. And so the ball was on my side of the court, and I served it back with a phone call to Ann and some talk and assurances. "Oh, I know you," she said. "You used to play guitar on your back porch. I could hear you from Grandma's house."

"Oh, yes," I assured her, "I was and am that guy, and I remember so well how striking you were that day we practiced at your grandma's." I was clutching at threads of connection. Finally I invited her to see a movie together, just the two of us at an early showing and she could pick the movie. My sincerity must have risen above my desperation, because she agreed, and with my reading the newspaper listings to her over the phone, we set the time and film.

Another absurdity came when I borrowed my Uncle Harry's nice DeSoto car and knocked at Grandma Ferroni's door. Ann did not come out this time, but her mother did, and she told me, "Oh, we don't live here anymore. We moved to a new house up on Garfield." She motioned with her hand as I apologized, then she said, "I'll take you there if you want." And so my date for the moment was her mother who admired my nice clean car. When I told her it was my uncle's, she laughed, "Oh, I know Harry. I went to school with him. He was such a nice boy." And so with the clean car and nice boy uncle I scored two points toward acceptance. I had been warned that Sue, Ann's mother, was strict about Ann's dating boys. I tried to show her I was a gentleman.

At their house on the corner of Garfield and Sinclair, I was taken through a spotless kitchen to a seat on their mohair couch. John, her father, in a white shirt, entered to meet me. I had seen John often on the bus coming home from his mill job, and always in a white shirt and slacks, sometimes a suit coat European style. "I'll get you a nice drink of orange," Sue said. "Annie will be right out." John and I sat in silence a few moments, and then she appeared. Wearing a beautiful dark blue dress with a white lace collar, her dark hair up and her hazel eyes sparkling, she walked toward me. I rose immediately.

"Oh, hi," she said smiling and taking my hand. "I hear you went to Grandma's house." This was unlike any of the other girls I'd dated and all so wonderfully nice. Her voice was the music for the movie we were in.

"Yeah, thank goodness for your mom," I said and meant it. I would not have missed meeting Ann for the world. Sue handed me a tall glass of orange drink which I'm sure I downed too fast, so eager to be alone with Ann.

On the way to the Paramount Theater in Steubenville, we talked of mutual friends and of school. Ann was going into her last year of nursing school at the Wheeling North Hospital, and I would be a senior at Muskingum. What I noticed was her politeness and confidence. I was thankful for the bench seats in the car and wished she would slide closer, but I was not about to force anything with this girl. More than a girl, she was a beautiful young woman, easy to talk with and somehow aware of people and ideas in the nicest way. At some point, she said she loved chocolate sodas, and I promised her one that night.

The film we had selected was *The Carpetbaggers,* a Southern saga loosely based on the life of Howard Hughes and Jean Harlow with George Peppard and Carroll Baker in the leads. It was romantic but in a sad way as the main characters created more ruin than good. At some point when the Hughes character failed to connect with the woman, I whispered to Ann, "The man's problem is he doesn't know how to love." She smiled and her hand drifted over mine. Later she would tell me that I had won her with that line. But it was no line, for I had experienced it myself. At two hours and thirty minutes, the movie ran long, and I had promised to get Ann a soda and home by 10:00.

"What shall we do?" I asked on the way to the car. "I'm having such a great time."

"I know," she said, "but I don't want to upset my mother. Let's get the soda another time."

I was glad to trade for "another time" with her. And so we arrived at her front door precisely at 10. On the way home we had made plans to go to a nice restaurant in Wheeling the next evening. Standing there, breathing in the shadows, I didn't want to release her hands, and she didn't pull away but leaned toward me for a sweet good-night kiss.

My head may have been spinning as I drove the car back to Uncle Harry's garage, but I know for certain that my heart was on fire.

We began seeing each other as much as possible that summer, going to plays like *Showboat* done along the river in a huge paddle boat, then *South Pacific* in the Pittsburgh Convention Center. Though she had dated little, Ann was aware and alive to art and music and to films and good writing. Where had she been all those years? I had dated only Barbara for six years. It was exciting, and with a nice summer income from the mill, we enjoyed the movies, parks and lakes. Meals at her house were a delight with Sue piling the food upon my plate, pasta yes, but also "Have some chicken. Take more salad. Eat."

By the end of summer, I had earned enough to talk of buying a car, and Dad was willing to go half on it with me. That drive to Muskingum must have worn him down. We found a $1,000 car in Wheeling, a small 1960 Fiat sedan, powder blue and white with four doors. In a steel valley like ours, a foreign car was quite unique and not well liked, but it ran well and looked really sharp for my Italian girlfriend. I bonded with that car as I had with Ann. It would be my way to school and back on weekends to pick her up in Wheeling and drive home to Mingo together. She began to learn to drive stick by shifting the gears for me as we rolled along the West Virginia hillside up the broad Ohio. The car was also our place to romance on the hills overlooking the valley. Though our passions grew, steaming up the windows at times, our respect for each other and what we felt remained steady. We wrote each other back and forth from schools, sharing our worlds and making plans.

By Christmas that year, I had saved enough by working in the cafeteria to buy an engagement ring, and so, before evening Mass, we drove out to a private road where I asked Ann to open the Fiat's glove compartment. A small box with a blue ribbon was opened, and she smiled and whispered "Yes" with a kiss. In a swirl of happiness we both laughed and cried. Later when we showed the ring to her mother, Sue nodded and smiled slightly, then said sternly, "I'm going to do what my father did to John." Ever so deliberately she added, "I don't have a rope like my father used to threaten John, but I have a knife in the basement, and if you are not good to her," and she leaned close to my face, "I swear I'll use it on you." I tried to find a face to assure her that I loved Ann and would protect her. Then Sue looked at Ann and said, "And you better be good to him too." We had passed the rite of engagement in that house, and it all felt good. After a shower of incense during Mass we walked down to my parents' house. Mom was still awake in the kitchen, and when we told her, she smiled and just said, "Well, that's nice." So Ann showed her the small diamond ring, and Mom gasped. "Oh my gosh! So you do mean it, you're really engaged?" Yes, we cried and hugged some more.

*   *   *

Things were going well that fall semester of 1964. My English major was complete, and I was doing my student teaching at Cambridge High School to a freshman and sophomore class. I would earn my teaching certificate for secondary schools. Part of who I was then and remain today is a teacher. Though often quiet at parties and events, in the classroom I spark with life, making quick observations, catching intentions, and making dialogue while also sensing the room and the timing. I grew up in a family where boredom was not practiced. However, that first day of teaching I had over prepared, doing detailed lesson plans and actually memorizing what I would say each moment. I soon learned that real education doesn't happen that way. You must be alive to the moment. Though I had much to learn, I sensed that I was connecting with my students' struggles to learn. I had been there myself.

The next semester I began to interview for teaching jobs around the state. On one fieldtrip our Teaching Methods class drove to Euclid High School outside of Cleveland where we learned the method of small group discussions. It was a fine progressive school system, and to my amazement a half a year later I would be teaching there myself.

The spring of 1965, I was having some car troubles, so I hitched a ride home with a college friend. Around 5 pm I borrowed Dad's new Chevy and headed to Wheeling to pick up Ann, but I never made it. Halfway down Route 7 the right wheels slid off the road into a gravel ditch, a tire blew, and the steering took me far left across the center and clear off the road. The last thing I remember was a huge tree and then blackness followed by a sense of the car rolling over in slow motion once, twice, and stopping on its side. When I awoke I could hear the Ohio River near me. Before me were deep brush and small trees and the lights of traffic above going north. With my legs pinned out the door, all I could do was turn on the headlights and lay onto the horn. Within minutes cars stopped, and I could hear voices coming near me. They were deciding what to do. Three men tilted the car partway, while another, John, pulled me out the door and onto my feet. The car crashed over sending me chills. With help I made it through the rubble to the road. John would take me to the hospital in Steubenville. I was dazed and amazed. Fifteen minutes ago I had thought I was dead and now I was alive.

On the road to the hospital we talked little. I think I was in disbelief or some kind of shock, but when we neared the exit to Mingo, I called out, "Wait. That's my parents' house." We veered off and John went to knock at the door. Dad came rushing out, Mom and sister Debbie stared out from the porch. Dad looked me over, then talked with them and got in the back of John's car to ride with us to the Ohio Valley Hospital. I tried my best to tell him what had happened, helped by John. When I attempted to get out of the car at the Emergency Room, I went down on my knees. I had walked from the car to the road, but now I could not stand on my left leg. A wheelchair came out to usher me in. I remember saying, "Someone needs to tell Ann. Someone needs to call at her school."

"Take it easy, son" Dad kept saying. "Take it easy. Someone will."

I was stripped down and given a hospital gown and something for the pain. I just lay there a while outside any sense of time as they examined me. I heard the words "broken," "x-rays," "Dr. Mancini" and was about to pass out. They all left, and Dad was watching over me, when for no sane reason, I joked, "You know, I never really liked that car." I had just destroyed my father's new car and dared to joke about it. In the days ahead I would apologize again and again.

When Mom arrived with Ann, they found me lying in a hospital bed out in the hallway, and we all were brought to tears. Though I was in pain and would be for some time, I was strangely grateful—that I was still alive, that something or someone had been watching over me, and that those I loved were near. After several days I went home on crutches and with a full-leg cast that bent at the knee. I was wounded but whole. I thanked God for saving me, but for years I would avoid driving on that same roadway, fearful that my escape from death was only a brief reprieve.

I know that I was changed in ways from nearing death, but what I was to learn from it all was still growing inside of me. I had not closed the door on God and religion, only opened it wider. Once around 12 years old, while in church waiting for my dad, brother, and uncle to show up, I sat and focused on asking God for a sign. "Just show me something, if you expect me to believe. Show me in some way." Quiet and mindful I waited when midway through the sermon, I was moved, shaken, by a profound sense of presence. God was no longer separate but in the world and in me. When Dad looked at me, he whispered, "Boy, you are white. If you're sick you should leave." I wasn't sick, but moved deeply beyond comprehension, and I walked out amidst choir voices to almost run my way home to my room.

I told no one till decades later I wrote the poem "The Journey Home" (p. 226).

After the accident, to everyone's surprise, I was able to drive my little Fiat to and from campus, then I'd hobble on crutches to my classes. Castless in June, I crossed the stage to pick up my degree by using a cane for my weakened leg. Two weeks later I was hired again at Weirton Steel where foreman Bob gave me the easy job of cleaning the locker room for the first two weeks. Ann began practicing nursing at St. John's Hospital in Steubenville. Wedding plans were taking up much of our time together, as we negotiated agreements between our parents. During this time Ann and I began weekly instructions from a young priest. We would have a Catholic wedding but without a Mass; I would agree to raise the children in the Catholic faith. For my best man I asked my brother, with Kenny and Billy, and neighbor Marian as groomsmen. Ann would have all J's...Janis her roommate as maid of honor, Jeannie from nursing school, Janet her sister, and Janis my sister as bridesmaids.

On the wedding day, David and I walked up the street to enter St. Agnes Catholic Church. A light hangover from the night before was keeping us silent. Then outside the church he said, "Hey, here's my car keys if you still want to make an escape." I laughed knowing that he would have talked me out of such a wrong move. There we were, two protestant boys, standing quietly in the vestibule waiting and noting the bottle of communion wine. We both shook our head. We had had enough to drink.

Ann was just lovely in her wedding gown, as her tearful father brought her down the aisle. I thought I might have to wrestle him for her hand. We stood together and took our vows. This was the best thing I had ever done, and

I felt I could fly out of there with her in my arms. Her mother Sue had managed the receptions, including cooking wedding soup and spaghetti for 60 people right after the wedding, followed later by an evening reception with band and more food and drink. While I sat along the wall, Ann danced the bridal dance with the men at the hall, earning us enough money to pay for our two nights at Niagara Falls. We were blind in love, enjoying all, except the long wait to be off on our honeymoon.

That first night after struggling to get the door of the old motel open, we made love for the first time in New Philadelphia, Ohio, falling asleep holding each other. The next morning we went to Mass, had pancakes in a local diner, and bought an inexpensive Kodak camera to begin recording our life together. Later, crossing the border into Niagara Falls, Canada, we found our second motel home. It was a romantic site in 1965, not as touristy as today, good for daring the waters on the Maid of the Mist boats and for evening walks along the paths with the falls in rainbow colors. Back in the hotel we entered the waters of our first shower together. The next day we drove home as husband and wife.

A word about my mother-in-law Sue Ferroni Zaben, who deserves a book for her character and her story, the oldest daughter of nine, born of Italian immigrants to America. She was turned away from the public schools for being too small, though her age was right; then she attended the next year without knowing English. She faced the stereotyping and ugly bias against Italian Americans, and developed a huge chip on her shoulder toward "showing those Americans" that she and her family were alright— "just as good and better." Her withdrawing from school in the eighth grade was done to help out at home, serving as a second mother to most of her eight brothers and sisters.

Sue knew who she was and let others know she was not afraid, though I would watch her turn shy in unfamiliar crowds. Sue was also the family story teller in a family of talkers, and she could command the floor with her dramatic telling, making faces, banging on the table, pacing while raising and lowering her voice. Once when left in the kitchen alone hearing her story, I told her she was a real raconteur. She looked at me funny, till I explained, "No, you're a great story teller. I admire you. I wish I could tell stories like you do." And she thought a moment then replied, "And I wish I could write my stories like you, then I wouldn't have to keep telling them." Any trouble I would have winning Ann's independence would be with this strong woman. And yet Sue loved her older husband John, guarded over her girls, and trusted me, for which I am forever thankful.

Back at work on the Monday after our brief honeymoon, it was raining hard in the mill yard, so foreman Bob called us into an empty freight car. We sat for a while hearing the rain's sharp pounding on the roof, then Bob turned to me and asked, "Well, Larry, you're a married man now. So how was the honeymoon?"

I was struck with embarrassment as they all eyed me, and I threw back, "Well, Bob, how was your honeymoon? Can you still remember it?"

"Oh, yeah," Bob grinned. "I'll tell you. When I was first married, I used to reach over in our bed to find my wife." Light laughter, "And now," he added, "Everywhere I reach, I find my wife." Big laugh, and the pressure let up along with the rain.

Harder than all of the wedding plans was our finding a place to live for our three months in Steubenville. By late August we would be moving to Euclid, Ohio, where we both had jobs starting careers in nursing and teaching. Apartments in Steubenville were hard to find and pretty awful. One was down a dark hallway smelling of urine and ending in bare walls with a single hanging bulb for light, a step above being homeless. We began to wonder if we would have to live with our parents. But following the classifieds finally led us to secure an upstairs apartment on Steubenville's noisy Seventh Street above a music teacher and her old family. When we returned from our weekend honeymoon at Niagara Falls, they had done little to prepare the place, and my father and I had to haul a refrigerator up two flights from their basement. At night we faced a locked front door so that we had to knock to be let in, then walk past the old woman in her slip and her husband in his t-shirt sleeping on the couch. And yet for the first time in our lives we had our own place together. We worked hard that hot summer of transition, learning to cook and budget, and to accept each other. I was not writing then; my life was writing me.

When August came, we rented a U-Haul trailer, and with our small Fiat hauled it upriver, then up over the last Appalachian foothill heading due north toward Cleveland and that great Lake Erie.

Chapter Five: Starting Out—Married Life & Work

Raised in a small town and attending small schools, both Ann and I found ourselves in 1965 living in Euclid, Ohio, a dense suburban city of 60,000. She began nursing work as a recent graduate dealing with elderly patients, then moving from geriatrics to pediatrics. Her yearly salary matched my own at exactly—$4,500. Granted it was a step up from being a student, but it allowed for little more than necessities, a movie once a week, and money to drive home to Mingo every other weekend. As a young married couple still learning about each other, we often came home from work at the same time, embraced and cuddled up on the couch for a nap before dinner. We soon became familiar with the daily dinner specials at Perkins Pancake House across the street from our apartment, a new building within a block of Lake Erie. Except for a few hand-me-downs, our furniture was new. Somehow with $600 we bought a bedroom suite, a couch and tables, a kitchen table and chairs, all from the big Sears store in downtown Cleveland. Every month we would drive into the city to make our payment at the Sears building near University Circle.

Euclid High School had 3,000 students in three grades, and I was a member of the large English department, headed by Frank, who for some blessed reason had liked me enough to hire me. He also trusted me enough to assign me a spot on the junior English teaching team. Here, four teachers coordinated large group presentations and small group section work, much like a college course. We each had our set of 25 students to discuss readings with, assign papers to, and then grade. Writing was important here, as was classroom discussion. Big for me was that I had teaching colleagues to work with and learn from. They say the first three years of teaching are the hardest, but with these close colleagues it became much easier.

One of the signs of the times at the school was that there were two teachers' lounges, a Men's and a Women's, as though we couldn't be trusted together. Typical topics in the men's lounge were the Cleveland Indians and Browns, and, of course, salaries and assignments. Rumbles of striking could be heard from time to time. I often wondered what the women discussed.

At one point during my second year, I had suggested assigning J. D. Salinger's *The Catcher in the Rye* novel to juniors. This met with some controversy among my colleagues, and so Frank asked me to present it to the English department. The language was an issue for some, but we all knew our students talked like the main character. For others it was what they saw as the emptiness of the ending. "What does he learn?" Mildred asked. "How is Holden any better at the end of the book?" Yet the ending echoed my own college awakening to life's ambiguity and deep questioning as necessary steps toward finding one's true path. I humbly tried to express this to my colleagues, and thankfully was joined by others who cited works of literature and film that also ended with the setting aside of false patterns and untested truths. *The Great Gatsby*, a book that all English teachers loved and used was mentioned, as was *The Adventures of Huckleberry Finn*, a book we were all then teaching in American literature. Looking around the room I was moved by how we were having a real cultural discussion beyond any talk of budgets and room assignments. A vote was taken, and *A Catcher in the Rye* made it onto an optional list for junior English.

One of the other great things about Euclid High was the encouragement to take graduate courses in the summers, which included raises for each class taken. And so I enrolled at Kent State University and began my graduate studies and inching my way up the pay scale. Three days a week, I would drive the hour down to Kent, Ohio, and learn from some of the fine teachers there. I think if I had been teaching at one of my other job offers at rural Ohio schools, I would never have done this and so become stagnant in my teaching career. I remember one of the older teachers at Euclid telling me once that "The only way to get through this teaching work is to come in on Monday and point your nose towards Friday." I did not believe him. More practical advice came from Frank who told me, "Listen, a word. Buy two suits, one blue and one gray, and you can wear them as suits or mix and match. No one will know the difference." I also learned to drop the college sarcasm with students when I told a young girl who kept missing exams, "You know, Louise, you're more trouble than you're worth." Ouch, that was met by her real tears and my guilt. Gradually I was becoming a real teacher even as I was moving towards graduate school.

Socially the world at that time was becoming more turbulent and violent. In 1966, soon after we arrived in Euclid, fiery racial riots erupted in the Hough area of downtown Cleveland and were met with the National Guard encampment. Ann and I drove past the tanks and troops in Rockefeller Park on our way to pay Sears. In 1965 the U.S. began bombing North Vietnam, then sending in combat troops to that war which would last a decade from 1965-1975. While many of my high school friends were being drafted or enlisting, I had had a student deferment while in college, then I was deferred for teaching in a large urban setting. Finally I would become a "Kennedy Father" with the birth of our daughter Laura in July of 1967.

Her birth had not come easy, though we had been planning for it from our wedding. Waiting those two years was probably wise. We had moved by then into Blisswood Homes, older two level row houses, sometimes called the "baby mill." Here we developed friendships with our neighbors, sharing babysitting and home entertaining with board games and good talk. It felt like the old neighborhood again. When Laura was born that July 24th, 7 days late, Ann's mother and mine drove up to be with us. We greeted our baby girl in the nursery together. Ann had been given a spinal, and subsequently had a strong headache for days. That night, my neighbor Rolly took me out to celebrate at the local pub. He also drove me home after I had deeply imbibed in shots and beers, so that I greeted my mother and Ann's with a big grin, hugged them both generously, then crashed on the couch. Four days later, we brought little Laura Jean Smith home to her white bassinet in our bedroom, which we could rock from our bed. She had expanded our nuclear family in a big way. I was now a father and Ann a mother, though it would take years to understand what all that meant, and it would be ever changing as she grew.

Our reasons for leaving our cozy cove in Euclid and our jobs were complex. Enthused by the challenge and rewards of real literary study, the thought of teaching on a college level drew me. But there was also the tedium of high school teaching, monitoring study halls, the cafeteria, and the hallways between classes. I once ran down a boy with his shirt tail out, entered his classroom and shouted to the teacher, "He has his shirt untucked!" Clearly I was losing it. I hated that policing work really. That year school girls had to wear skirts that would touch the ground if they kneeled, and didn't the principal dare to enforce this once by having a young girl kneel on the floor before him. Her mother came in the next day in a flurry of protest, and that rule was forgotten along with shirt tail tucking.

Another taste of absurdity came for me in 10th period study hall (we actually had 10 periods in the day). On this particular day I was monitoring the students sitting in the auditorium to be sure they were working and not sleeping. I would confront them with, "Okay, you, sit up and open a book." On this day when I rounded the front of the room, my back was hit by something solid. I looked down to the ground and there lay the biggest gob of chewing gum I had ever seen. They had literally joined together in this protest. I looked around and walked out into the hallway. The students were hating me for doing a job I too hated. I was becoming an absurd caricature of myself. I knew Holden Caulfield would call us all "phony bastards" for this enforced attention. My stomach sickened, I had to escape this trap. Ann's uncle Chuck had made this transition from high school to college teaching a year before me. And so that summer of 1968, with Ann's agreement to continue nursing in a hospital near Kent, we packed up and moved to Kent, Ohio. Here I could earn my Masters and eventually my Doctorate in English literature.

We found a duplex apartment a half mile south of campus where families from the town and the college lived together. Uncle Chuck and his kids helped us move. The place needed a great deal of cleaning up after the last bunch of college students, but we agreed to it. Hard work was part of our way of being and surviving. While living there we also got our first rescue dog, named Snoopy by Laura. Still a pup, he ate shoes and purses, fishing rod handles, and old books stored in the basement. Ann was hired right away at Robinson Memorial Hospital in Ravenna, and I was busy taking summer classes when we learned that Ann might be pregnant. We were counting on her salary, and so in desperation I went in to see the chairman of the Graduate English Department. Dr. German heard my story, read my average scores on the graduate record exam, but was most impressed that I had already taught English in the public schools. "I'll see what I can do," he said, and the next day, I was called and told I had a graduate assistant-ship. When I asked what this meant, the secretary said, "Well, your classes are free now and you'll receive a stipend of $1,200 this semester." When I asked what I was to do for it, she said, "We'll call and let you know soon." Fall classes were to start in two weeks. I shared the good news with Ann, and waited.

The day before classes were to start, I got the call. I would be teaching a freshman English class the next morning at 10:00 a.m. I was in some sort of shock upon hearing this, but in talking with my neighbor and graduate fellow, Pat, he assured me that I could do it, "Just take attendance, go over the syllabus which the department provides, and let them go. It'll give you two days to get something together." And that is how I began my college teaching career on the fly. When I took the "Introduction to Teaching" class later that week I realized that I was way ahead of the others in terms of methods. Most had come right from college graduation and didn't know of lesson plans or what an overhead projector was or how to work it. I showed them and did well in the classroom.

Two weeks later, Ann got her period, but the crisis had jump-started my college teaching career. As at Muskingum, there were some fine teachers at Kent, some wrapped up in their research and reputation as scholars, and some who were also fine human beings. Glenn Burne, in comparative literature, was inspiring for the way he made literature relevant. He would begin with a text by

Franz Kafka or Albert Camus and at some point take off his sports coat, maybe roll up his sleeves, and get down to brass tacks with working on the text, tying it to our world and our lives. The writing mattered. Besides introducing me to some wonderful writers, he modeled how to be an engaged teacher. While some of the professors were territorial and often snide about each other, he was open and sought to see connections with other writings and studies. Sanford Marovitz was also a favorite and served as a strong yet generous advisor for both my masters' thesis on writer Sherwood Anderson and later on my doctorate dissertation on Kenneth Patchen.

The crisis at Kent State came for the whole campus and town and the world. By May 4, 1970, after five days of campus protests against President Nixon's ordering troops into Cambodia, someone(s) set fire to the old ROTC barracks building on campus. Protests and reprisals went back and forth for a day, then everything was suddenly escalated into a noon rally on the campus Commons. Ohio's National Guard was ordered onto campus by then Governor James Rhodes. They had been standing at a strike in Akron, and some were Kent students. Protesters gathered on the Commons with signs and shouting. When the troops began pushing the students back, they began throwing words and some rocks at the troops. An order was suddenly given to fire into the students, and the guardsmen lowered their rifles, then fired 67 rounds over a period of 13 seconds, killing four students and wounding nine others, including one who suffered permanent paralysis. It all became a national disaster known as the Kent State Massacre. Sympathetic student protests and strikes occurred around the country, resulting in many campuses shutting down and further killings of two black students at Jackson State University in Mississippi.

For days we had watched the smoke clouds over the campus and heard the warping beat of helicopters patrolling the campus and surrounding area, yet we had never expected such a violent result. The day of the shootings, I was at home with daughter Laura playing in the yard. When our neighbor Anna came knocking at the door, I came around the corner to see her startled face. "Oh, Larry," she said almost hysterical, "They are shooting our students!" We held each other a moment then each of us got our children and dog into the house. I turned on the television and radio hoping for news. Within minutes the phone rang. It was Ann at work in Ravenna. "Are you guys alright?" she asked, her voice shaking. Though the news reports were all of the guardsmen being wounded, Ann said tearfully, "Oh, no, it's all students they are bringing in, all wounded and some of them...dead. It's so awful and sad."

That night while Laura slept, we sat together with our grief, our disbelief, and our anger, uncertain of our world and future.

When the war first started under Jack Kennedy's administration, Ann and I had remained neutral. Sheltered by my deferments, I lacked a voice. But when Lyndon Johnson advanced us further into the war and we began learning of the wounds and deaths it inflicted on so many people, including friends and family, we began writing letters, signing petitions, and speaking out among family against the war. However, the experience of Kent State radicalized us in new and deeper ways. The town of Kent was split between campus and town on this issue. What we kept hearing quoted from some was that the damage the students had done to buildings brought on their own punishment. We could not accept this. People mattered more than property. You don't shoot random students for the acts of a few, many outside agitators. Next, the campus was closed down under martial law and the students were sent home. One of my students, Tod, whose father came to pick him up, was angry at the students. Tod wrote to me, "'Those students got what they deserved,' he kept saying. And, Larry, I spoke up, 'But, Dad, I was one of those students.' And my dad said to me, 'Well, then maybe you should have been shot.' My own father!" This values split was clearly dividing this country and families.

In truth, for some time Ann and I could not easily speak of the shootings of that day, our grief was so fresh and our distrust of being understood by listeners so strong. By the end of that summer my course work was done, and I could at last get a full-time job teaching while finishing my dissertation. After getting a lot of rejections at four year colleges, I began sending my resume to branch campuses and community colleges. Though my beard and hair were trimmed, the fact that I was coming from Kent State University did me no good when applying for a position. Finally I received a request for an interview from Bowling Green State University's Firelands College located in Huron, Ohio, where my family had vacationed all those summers. I drove up to Bowling Green and the main campus for the first interviews, then I drove over to Huron with the instruction, "You keep driving past corn and soy bean fields, and finally in the middle of one, there will be a two red brick buildings. That's Firelands College." Though there was some truth to that, after a year I grew to resent the main campus bias and the nick name of mini-Bowling Green.

That day, I was interviewed by the dean, who fortunately had graduated from Muskingum College, then by the three member English Department. They were impressed with my having taught three years of high school English and my work with writing. I left the room with their, "Thank you, and we'll let you know." At the end of the hallway I stopped. I wanted this job. I needed it to support my family. I went back and told them that I promised to do a good job if hired. As I was leaving the building I ran into Ray, another teaching fellow from Kent. "Hey," he said.

"Hey, to you," I said and shook hands with him. There was a pause, then I said, "If I don't get it, I hope you do," and he granted me the same well wish.

Besides the atmosphere surrounding the Kent State shootings, two other life changing events occurred...one short and one extended, but both long lasting. In 1968 when I was a fresh graduate student of Kent's English Department, a visiting author came to campus. Gary Snyder was a young ponytailed American Buddhist and fellow traveler with the Beat authors, Jack Kerouac and Allen Ginsberg. He was also a rebel spirit, with contemporaries like Michael McClure and Philip Whalen. In a seminal way, his energetic and grounded talk and readings on campus opened the door for me both as a scholar and as a writer. Again the dawning awareness came, "So, there can be writing like this!"

In an academic room of 100 persons, Snyder's intimate yet universal sharing of experience and values in a moving form was stirring. He was not just making literature; he was living it. As he declared, "As a poet I hold the most archaic values on earth. They go back to the upper Paleolithic: the fertility of the soil, the magic of animals, the power-vision in solitude, the terrifying initiation and rebirth, the love and ecstasy of the dance, the common work of the tribe. I try to hold both history and wilderness in mind, that my poems may approach the true measure of things and stand against the unbalance and ignorance of our times." (David Kherdian, *Six Poets of the San Francisco Renaissance: Portraits and Checklists* (1967), p. 52.) When Kent's campus, if not the world, seemed to fall apart after the shootings, this holistic vision was reassuring. Fellow graduate student and poet Maj Ragain recalls this visit by Snyder as equally transforming and sustaining of both life and art. Snyder's writing and example have guided many, including me most of my life.

The third life changing experience at and after Kent State was the research work I was doing on author Kenneth Patchen. His working-class roots in the steeltowns of Warren and Youngstown certainly drew me as in this poem:

The Orange Bears: Childhood in an Ohio Steeltown

> The Orange bears with soft friendly eyes
> Who played with me when I was ten,
> Christ, before I'd left home they'd had
> Their paws smashed in the rolls, their backs
> Seared by hot slag, their soft trusting
> Bellies kicked in, their tongues ripped
> Out
> . . . .
>
> I remember you would put daisies
> On the windowsill at night and in
> The morning they'd be so covered with soot
> You couldn't tell what they were anymore.
> A hell of a fat chance my orange bears had!

This open confrontation and lament calls out for recognition and reform. It called to me as a brother would. Patchen made art of working peoples' lives and refused to accept the unjust status quo. Like fellow Ohioan James Wright, they made a poetry of my place and people. Also Patchen's taking a maverick position in the world of writing and publishing was inspiring. He never made the same book twice, nor turned art into commercialism. And he found means of getting past any publishing walls by creating a way around them. He is perhaps America's most prolific rebel poet. Though my own writing is less daring and innovative, Patchen's life and work set out a viable example for finding my own stance. I also came to love research by working on his biography. Most of it was original...finding and scouring his correspondence, interviewing family and fellow artists, travelling to his and wife Miriam's many places in Greenwich Village, New York; Norfolk and Old Lyme, Connecticut; Warren, Ohio; and San Francisco and Palo Alto, California. His world enlarged my own and opened new ways of viewing and making an engaged writing that mattered not just to academics, but to all.

Just as at Muskingum, I found new pathways of using my training as a scholar and writer to bring respect, recognition, and perhaps understanding, to the working-class world of my life and others.

Chapter Six: Life Along the Lake

Ann and I again found ourselves struggling to find an adequate place to live, this time in Huron, Ohio, a small residential town along the lake shore. It seemed almost a suburb of the city of Sandusky and a summer tourist site along the busy trail to the Cedar Point Amusement Park. Here were many houses but few for rent and almost no apartments in 1970. That summer we had been house-sitting in Ashland, Ohio, for Ann's Uncle Chuck and Aunt Virginia, while they toured the country in a camper. Our furniture was all stored in their garage. Many days Ann worked in the Ashland hospital while Laura, I, and our dog Snoopy would drive north in search of our next home. This was working out fine until Chuck and Virginia and their three kids came home a month early, making our search for a house imperative.

We found that we had to buy, which was something new and unexpected. We couldn't and wouldn't pay a kingdom, but, yes, we did need to buy. With no real savings, we would cash in my three years of teacher's retirement payments. Our realtor Joan pulled a listing from her drawer and took us to a summer cottage a block from the lake. It had that rustic ¾" pine paneling in every room, a living room with a fireplace, and two small bedrooms. When Ann's sister visited and walked from the house to the large sandy beach, she gasped, "Oh, you *have* to buy this house!" My father's advice was more practical, "Good construction but the house and lot are mighty small." On the other side of bank dealings, we found ourselves as homeowners, except for our mortgage of $16,000.

Well, we had jobs, or at least we thought so. Ann was signed on at Good Samaritan Hospital in Sandusky right away, but I hadn't heard from the college in more than a month. The old insecurities kicked in, and so I made a sheepish call to the college, "Hi, this is Larry Smith. I think I'm your new English teacher. Can you check?" The secretary laughed, then took a moment to check and confirm. I thanked her and sighed relief. The town had the Huron River dividing it, a grocery store on each side, a harbor for shipments of grain, limestone, and iron ore, and a scattering of marinas and good restaurants. We realized by the summer traffic that we were now living in vacationland and, though we would come to resent the traffic, we knew the amusement park meant work for many folks, including my students. We fished the long pier to the lighthouse, rode bikes through tree lined neighborhoods, began to make friends of neighbors and colleagues. A favorite activity when family visited was to ride the transport ferries from Sandusky downtown over to Cedar Point Marina, land-lubbers daring the seas and feeling the wind and splash of lake waves. When the entrance price to the park rose dramatically, I'm afraid we would torture our children by just taking the boat ride, walking around the marina at the Point's portside then board the next boat back. We couldn't afford to live like the tourists. We were slowly becoming a part of the place and it a part of us.

Over time Huron proved to be deceptively stratified by economics into a series of beach neighborhoods with no connecting streets. At gatherings we watched as others from Huron questioned of newcomers, "So, where do you live?" Answer and you would be classified. The richest area lay to the eastern edge of town at Beachwood Cove, next came middle-class Chaska Beach, and then Old Homestead, where we lived. The western part of town and our Old Homestead area were home to educated working-class families with children and with neighbors who seemed welcoming. That first week, Old Jack next door invited me into his garage where his tools were neatly displayed. "Come and borrow them anytime," he said, "You don't have to ask." Throughout town, lawns were kept and maple trees lined the streets. Across the Huron River bridge, past the large docks, one came into the old town, three story lake homes on quiet streets, and then a series of newer housing developments. At the edge of most Midwest towns suddenly are fields and farms, and Huron was no exception. In fact that is where the college and my future work lay.

Downtown Huron was suffering the demise of old Main Street for an urban renewal project—the boat basin, which was and would remain only partially completed. It was a safe town where the police blotter contained such crimes as tape deck taken from car, a broken window in school building, man charged with dog running. That latter would be me when our yard dog had to be leashed at all times. Snoopy would often escape the yard and end up outside some neighbor's house where a female dog might be in heat. On one occasion when he returned to our back yard, I grabbed him by the collar and put him in the house. When a Huron policeman came around the corner asking where my dog was, I answered, "Why he's right there safe in the house." The policeman stared at him looking out of our French doors, and back at me. He said, "Yes, that's him, and I've been chasing that dog for the last 20 minutes." I smiled as he wrote me the ticket for "dog running" and gave me the court date. A week later I showed up to plead "no contest" and to try to explain. After all the DUI's and petty thefts were run through court, I pleaded and begged circumstances; the fine was dismissed, but not the court costs. Looking around the courtroom that day I learned that all sorts of folks were living in Huron, not just middle and upper class.

The students at the campus were from all of the surrounding small towns, both urban and rural. There were no dorms, so all had separate lives at home, and many worked full time to pay bills and for their own education. The age range was wide and challenging, but more like life than the restricted world of a youth-only residential college. I was their bearded teacher, only a few years older and younger than some. One fellow working at the large Ford plant in Lorain asked me before the whole class, "Say, how much do you make as a professor?" I told him I was not a professor but an instructor. He ignored this and got to his real point, "I bet I make more than you do." I smiled and said, "I bet you do." Then refusing to be totally defeated in this contest of jobs, I asked, "And how many hours a week do you have to be at your work?" He didn't answer. I grinned and for the purposes of that discussion did not mention the long hours away from family spent grading papers, preparing classes, or serving on committees. On another day, we went around stating our career goals, and one young man said, "I hope to be a tool and die maker." Then there was a young woman who wanted to be a nurse, and then a guy in his late 20s announced, "I am a tool and die maker, and one day I'll be a criminal layer." The two men stared at each other.

I soon began to see more purpose in my work. Most students were finding their way, and I was there to do more than teach writing and usage. I would expose them to life through literature and personal writing. I will admit that I took the job at Firelands College thinking, "This is a good place to start, but after a few years with a doctorate degree in hand, I'll move on to a four year private college." That dream never happened, and over the years I came to accept the rightness of my role of being at this place and opening its doors to so many first generation college students, just like myself.

Though I and many others hired in 1970 stayed on to teach for decades, others would come and go, much as they had in college and graduate school. Their jobs might end, better opportunitie might appear, some were let go after five years because they had not attained the doctorates. But that did not keep Ann and I from getting close to other couples. It worked best when both couples knew and liked each other. Eventually we helped others move in and move out when the time came. When close friends Patty and Mike moved on to jobs in Maine, I helped Mike load his U-Haul truck. We sat on the back end and Mike lamented, "Gheez, this van is only half full. I can't believe that after four years of marriage, this is all the stuff I own." I laughed aloud, and told him, "You're lucky, my friend. Ann and I own so much 'stuff' now, that moving anywhere seems impossible."

Yet when we sought to become part of the town community, we encountered some resistance because we were viewed as strangers, transient and perhaps over educated. Many of the oldest families here had come to the Firelands area following the American Revolutionary War when homes were burned down in Connecticut by British soldiers, and so survivors were given property in our Western Reserve—thus the Firelands name, though the fires had been elsewhere. With that migration to the Ohio area came a New England insularity that was alienating for newcomers, like us. One older woman explained, "Sorry, but you will have to live here 40 years before you are truly accepted." We shook our heads at this, but she added, "Oh, your kids will be accepted long before you because they have grown up here." More and more we found ourselves in university friendships or groups of fellow "outsiders" seeking community. While gossip still ran strong, as in Mingo, there was much more striving for status and upward mobility.

By the time our son Brian was born n 1972, Ann had gained an associate degree, and eventually a Bachelor's degree in nursing. She really felt that she needed a degree to feel equal with our college colleagues, and she worked hard to earn it. Though she also worked hard to bring natural childbirth to the area, by the time Brian was born, I was allowed back in the delivery area yet ushered away when he was born with a loud cry from Ann. Within two days, we brought our boy home. At one point after Brian was born, Ann sold Avon products in the neighborhood, often pushing baby Brian in a stroller. Eventually childcare arrangements were worked out by sharing the daycare of our children with other couples at the college. Our standard of parenting came from our family but also from our education. Ann was studying families and counseling directly, and I was learning much through reading the hundreds of personal essays I assigned and evaluated.

In a couple of years, when the two bedroom house seemed too cozy, we began looking for a nice larger home. Our realtor friend Joan helped us locate a Cape Cod one neighborhood over. It actually had four bedrooms, which proved essential as Ann was pregnant with our daughter Suzanne, born in December of 1975. Almost a bicentennial baby, she was a blonde blue-eyed bundle. A surprise baby or "love child" like myself, she was born while Ann was yet completing her master's degree in nursing. Like so many times in our life, we faced this bump in the road directly and so learned from it. We were now a family with working-class values living in a middle class neighborhood. Though our families lived several hours away, they never let us down when needed. Family mattered and was extended to close friends.

Chapter Seven: Other Journeys & Family Matters

By 1980, we had experienced the death of Ann's father John and of my maternal grandmother Jean Putnam, he from a stroke, she from cardiac arrest. Both took an emotional toll on us. Life was beginning to seem a trail of work, passing relationships, and deaths, counterbalanced by the growth of our children and the closeness of friends. Then in 1980-1981 we leaped into a transforming adventure. Our families supported our decision to move to Italy and the island of Sicily where I would teach for a year in the Fulbright program. The decision was agreed upon by us and our young children to welcome a year of adventure. Our jobs and schools, even our house and cars, had to be released for a nine month sojourn abroad. In August we all boarded a plane to another land with another language where we would, if not thrive, at least survive for a year. It was a brave undertaking and involved leaving the support group of our family and friends. Together with the university sabbatical half pay and the Fulbright fellowship we would venture it together. We flew to Rome where, after a week of training and adjustment while living in a spare hotel room, we boarded a train headed south to Catania, Sicily.

Here I would be teaching a course in "American Romanticism and the Beat Movement" with professor Maria Victoria DiAmico. Our three children would attend Italian schools and be tutored at home. They each took to the new country in their own way, Suzanne (4), the petite blonde Americano, was a favorite at preschool. Brian (8) found welcoming friends in fourth grade, and Laura (12) in junior high learned the language even better than her Italian-

American mother. Ann was our Italian speaker though; I, the reader. As another American teacher in Sicily pointed out, "Your kids are so fortunate. They get to experience being a minority." We all came to know the mixed blessing of that condition.

Fortunately we settled in a small town along the coast, yet we were clearly living on a different plane for that year, at times it seemed almost a different planet, though we came to love and respect the people and place. That journey truly broadened our world, and Laura and I each kept journals of it, some of mine turning into poems. Each day was an adventure in survival. I recall one memorable trip to Syracusa after we had been in Sicily for a couple months and were missing our English language and home. On the crowded bus driving back to Aci Castello, the fishing village where we lived, over the speakers came John Denver singing "Take me home, country roads./ To the place I belong..." Standing there holding the strap with one hand and Brian's hand with the other, my eyes filled with tears. Ann was looking across at me and we both just nodded. On another day while sitting in my university office I picked up my first book of poems, *Growth.* As I heard my American voice in those poems I was deeply moved by feelings of self and home.

The strain of assimilation with learning and thinking in a different language and grasping different customs weighed on us at times. Yet we all, including the children, gained a knowledge of other ways of living and being; this acceptance of others remains a part of us. Early on we sensed that most Sicilians saw us as rich American tourists, but as we lived with them and shopped for fresh fish and bread alongside of them, and sat with them in church, their warmth and welcome helped us to survive. Our Italian neighbor and counterpart, Peppino Paxia, his wife Maria, and their four children had lived in Canada on a similar teaching program and proved life-savers to us in so many ways. They were there for driving our kids to school, assisting us in buying an old Fiat car and the best cheese and wine, for listening to us and helping us find the humor of our adventure. Peppino told of a colleague from Canada who had so enjoyed the pesto sauce of Italy, and when he went home he attempted to duplicate it, only to write back, "My friend, I tried to find the ingredients, but the basil wasn't your basil, and the cheese and the olive oil weren't Italian olive oil or cheese, and finally, my friend, the pesto wasn't pesto."

We knew that we were fortunate to be there living the real thing. Before we came home, I wrote the story of our journey including our reconnecting after 50 years with Ann's Ferroni family of Giolianova. That trip up north included viewing strikingly beautiful landscapes, ruins, and cities as well as having four flat tires and eventually facing the death of our old Fiat. We boarded a train and made our way home. Much like the island of Sicily, we became bonded as a family needing each other to survive. Yet when we returned to America and our friends would ask, "So how was your trip?" expecting us to answer, "Oh, fine. Just wonderful," we would nod yes, sure, yet know it was both hard and sweet, like their bread.

Ann did a remarkable job of keeping the family going, getting food on the table, the children to schools, celebrating the day's togetherness, while I struggled to help and to get things done for my class. At the university we read Walt Whitman, Henry David Thoreau, Ralph Waldo Emerson, and then leaped into the Beat writing of Jack Kerouac, Allen Ginsberg, Gregory Corso, and my favorite, of course, Gary Snyder. At one point I had my students writing Japanese haiku in Italian and English. As the sole

American in the classroom, I would read aloud each author in my American voice. However, my own American writing voice was strangely transformed by constantly trying to think and speak in Italian. Even after we returned home at the beginning of the summer of 1981, I found myself living in America yet still struggling to come up with Italian expressions for situations. In truth, while I had gained great experience in Italy, I had neglected my creative writing and somehow lost touch with my native voice.

Back home we found we didn't have to travel to experience foreign cultures. Following our Fulbright year, we hosted two students from foreign countries. In 1984 it was Maryela Meza from Chile. In 1992 it was Esther Gonzalez from Spain. Both teenage girls were from divorced, often feuding families, had maids at home, yet were bright and loving. Blindly we had ignored that they were teenagers and that they would not necessarily get along with our children, though all loved little Suzanne. In our wish to "pay it back or forward" for our help abroad, we were making some large assumptions and causing some pretty major adjustments to our family dynamics. We were all finding our place with each other. One adjustment was the fact that these girls learned the American Midwest way of death in that my father died while Maryela was here, and my mother passed away during Esther's stay with us. When their time with us was up, we kissed at the airport and said, "Have a good life."

The tragic event of my father's passing from a cardiac infarction in 1984 would turn me back to my writing and lead to my work as a publisher. He had returned home from golfing with a friend and told my mother he was going to lie down. He took a couple cookies and a glass of milk upstairs. When he did not come down, Mom went up and found him on the bed. The rescue squad could not revive him, including his friend Brownie who told Mom, "I'm sorry, Jeanie, he's gone." I got the word while at a community meeting near us in Huron. Ann drove over and called me out of the meeting to give me the news in the hallway. I remember gasping, "No, oh God, no, it can't be!" My mother had been the one ill, and yet it was Dad who had died. Ann held me there and whispered comfort, then we drove home, gathered up our children and clothes and headed for our family in Mingo. Maryela Meza, our exchange student from Chile at the time, experienced death in an American family, as did we all.

Immediately, my mother went into a period of deep emotional denial, instructing us to gather their papers together and to share them with her again and again with our assurances: "Yes, things would be taken care of," when they did not feel that way at all for us. A dull persistent ache was running through my body. At the showing, many of his friends gathered, his old Boy Scouts, neighbors, church members and family, but not the railroaders he had worked with. My old friend Billy, then working as a train engineer, explained, "Railroaders are spooked by death." Mom continued to go through the motions without expressing her feelings. At the funeral it was surprisingly my uncle Harry who broke into tears for his younger brother and so released some of my own sorrow.

Following the funeral and the church basement wake, I stayed on for one of the hardest times of my life. Mom, still in denial, kept telling me to "Please just get rid of his things. I don't want to have to look at them." While concern for her had held me back emotionally during the funeral, now while I so wanted to hold onto everything about him, I was forced into removing them. Cousin Jeff and I hauled tools out of the basement for whomever wanted them, and boxes of his clothes went to the mission. Trash was taken to the landfill where we then piled it onto a fire in what seemed an insane act of cremation of all memories. Next, Mom and I made the rounds of the Social Security office and bank, where I would hear her numbly repeat, "My husband is dead. What do I do now?" Each word cut into me.

Finally, after a week of this hurting, I left Mom with my sister Debbie and headed home to grieve. I had forced down grief in order to do what was necessary. Yet, in our Volkswagen bus, halfway home past Tappan Lake where we had often fished, I had one of the strongest visions and revelations of my life. What came sweeping over me was Dad's presence in all things. He was with me everywhere, in the trees and lake waters, the wind against the van, the sound of the tires on the pavement, in the steering wheel I held to. Dad was there with me. I drove with this glowing feeling, laughing lightly through tears, for I knew he would be inside of me forever. The wall protecting me from mourning was gone, and I could begin to heal. Mystical or not, it was a spiritual experience. When I arrived home, Ann just held me in a loving embrace, as I tried to tell her my vision. For months I processed it through keeping a grief journal and talking with Ann.

As summer opened I took on the project of painting the outside of our house. Each day as I and the kids took up the brushes and worked the paint deep into the wooden face of the house, I touched the wound of loss, opened and released the feelings. If you can meditate a house, I did so that summer. Though it would take a year before I could write clearly of that pain, I was able to connect with my father's spirit and voice. He is sensed in "Things My Father Taught Me."

He moved with purpose
like the railroad. His hands

wore the calluses of work;
his eyes were dark pools of trust.
He taught with what he was,
with words like apples
sweet and tart—

"Trust the road
that takes you."
"Let the saw
do its work."
"The worst fear
is fear of work."
"Let the shovel
throw the dirt."

This year I wear his hat,
feel his touch inside this coat.
Inside my voice he speaks
of what it means
to be.

He loved with what he was.

The poem speaks this deep identification where he still had much to teach me about being who you are and about saying it straight. His life affected my life and my writing equally and still does. My painting of the house, so like his building of two houses, kept me near him and close to myself.

And then I set out on a trip to California where I was to research and write a book on "The San Francisco Renaissance in Poetry," which included both Kenneth Patchen and Lawrence Ferlinghetti and a host of other spirited writers. Not surprisingly I chose to take the railroad west and so boarded the Amtrak in Sandusky headed for Chicago and points west. Just out of Sandusky I realized the richness of this rail experience and kept a journal of the trip in both poetry and prose. For three steady days I felt the gentle rocking of the train, saw the visions of

towns and the backyards of factories, watched and felt the
tug of people inside the train, crossed the magnificent
Rockies, all while I read of the colorful and mythic sense of
the West Coast. While there, I stayed in the old Beat
Berkeley Hotel briefly until I found it overrun with bugs.
Each day I researched in Berkeley's Bancroft Library the
lives and work of California authors and their publications.
One memorable weekend I drove down the coast to Santa
Barbara on Route One in a Mustang convertible, sensing
again the mythic qualities of the coastal land and people.
While doing research I also worked on the long journal
poem which was to become my next book, *Across these
States: Journal Poems*. A few samples provide some sense
of its importance in my evolution as a person and a writer.

> All trains begin in Chicago.
> Chicago, monument of steel and glass—
> busy people grounded below.
> Newspaper sellers talk to air
> as people and pigeons shuffle across bridges.
>
> Train stopovers suck
> the life of a trip—
> marble monument of Union Station
> where people sit and stare, write postcards
> hang tight to luggage, fear the air.
> . . . .
> Towns of granaries and silos—
> Mendota, Illinois—trains
> Have always been here.
> Corn rows in Spring—
> from tender green inches
> of summer grain. Farmyards squared off
> like country cemeteries—
> and the train rocks, rocks me to sleep.
> Ann, when I open my eyes
> I see the landscape.
> When I close them
> I feel your face.

I think myself to sleep.

Upon arriving on the shores of the West Coast, I and the poem rise and close with these celebratory lines:

> At Stinson Beach girls laugh in surf
> and I take off my shoes and pants
> wade out waist deep.
> To be alive in this setting sun—
> ocean's roar at land's end—
> so many miles yet it seems like none.
> All a trip in the mind through time
> yet a being there as wordless
> as the juniper bush
> dripping with sun.
>
> I fill my cup, turn back to shore.
> We go on forever—
> there can never be enough.

During the trip and the writing I had made some transition from sadness into acceptance of my father's passing. I was witness here to life that embraced the darkness with the light. In a real concrete way my founding the press was building a publishing house as my father had built houses in Mingo. Bottom Dog Press has grown from a fine arts publisher of two to three small chapbooks a year, to publishing a total of 200 deserving literary books, eight to ten books per year. It has filled much of my life when not teaching or acting as a husband, parent, and grand-parent.

*   *   *

In the late 1980s we visited family in Mingo often to connect and to help out. Included in my *Milldust and Roses* is a long personal essay, "The Company of Widows," one of my most frequently published pieces which tells of a visit home to Mingo Junction with my wife and children. My mother was coming out of a year-long downward spiral emotionally where she struggled with depression and anxiety attacks, much of it due to wrong medications. On this one visit, a festival parade was going on in Steubenville, and so we picked up Ann's mother Sue and my mother Jean and headed uptown. My life and writing are clearly one in this piece which explores as it describes.

The Company of Widows

Every couple of months or so I return to the industrial Ohio Valley with its deep green Appalachian walls along that big winding river. And lately as I come into town bouncing over the gaping potholes of Steubenville streets, stopping at the traffic light beside that huge bridge to West Virginia, I stare at the new monument to the steel valley, a statue of a laborer in shiny asbestos suit frozen at that moment when he taps a sample from the blast furnace floor. He seems intent upon his job, only there is no blast furnace floor, just this laborer alone in time and space. I admire the statue's simple directness, its human scale and respect for reality. For me, this whole steel valley remains as real and fluid as the hot flowing iron of memory.

As I round the curve under the Market Street Bridge, my windows down to make a summer breeze, there is that aftertaste of something burnt in the air, and I swear you can taste it too in the water, as bittersweet as rust. Heavy barges of coal and ore move down river beside me as the gray air billows from smokestacks, rises and crests in a dark heavy cloud. I am enough of an outsider now to notice this; insiders never do, or if it gets too heavy and they are forced to cough each time they speak, they blame it on the milltown across the river—"Smells like Follansbee!" This place along the edge, so marked by extremes of beauty and waste, is my place, my hometown, my family—and I breathe and swallow it again.

"It ain't all bad," as they say, and I look over to see my wife awake now as we come into "Mingo Town." She smiles too at being home; my son looks up from his computer game at the blast furnaces that loom over the town, and we wake our twelve year old daughter, who asks, "Are we at Grandma's yet?"

I smile as the car winds up the steep hill, and pulls in before a yellow brick home. I unload our bags and leave everyone at Ann's mother's, then drive down St. Clair hill, staring into the steaming cauldrons of the mill. At Murdock Street I turn right, coast downhill, and pull in behind my mother's car. She has taken down the front maple, leafless for years, so that the whole place looks a little different and a whole lot the same—a three-story wooden frame house with worn green shingles along the edge of Ohio Route 7.

Mrs. Maul nods to me as I get out of the car— neighbors still, her yard still cared for like her retarded son who is now 33 and staring out the window at me. I wave then note how Mom's porch needs the mill dirt squirted off. I take the broom by the door, and start dancing it across the green painted concrete till she hears me, comes to the front window laughing, "Get in here, you nut."

It is at least a five minute wait as she wrestles her door locks, three of them where once there were none. But I don't object, I want her safe, and with the recent break-ins and thefts from cars, I tell her I will install another if she wants. "Don't worry," she says hugging me home, "We old girls keep an eye out for each other."

In Mom's house one never gets further than the "television room" where the set is always on. I've found her sleeping here some nights in her reclining chair in the glow of a snowy screen. We sit and she gives me news of who has died or been arrested, and word of my lost siblings; she offers me candy and a glass of root beer. She is sixty-four this year, my father's fatal heart attack upstairs, now three years past. Though we often speak of him, of what he'd think, of how he used to work so hard, of his joking with the kids, we never address his death. We both know that he is gone—the whole house echoes his absence, but we won't recall for each other those weeks around his death when we went through his things, sorting out tolls and clothes, taking papers from the mill to the Social Security office in Steubenville. It still breaks my heart remembering my mother sitting in that office, hearing her say to the stranger, "My husband's dead, now what do I do?"

Only this time as she brings in a plate of store-bought cookies, I am surprised to hear her say, "That day your dad died, he took a handful of these and a glass of milk. I remember, he said he was just going upstairs to lie down. He said he had to rest."

I cannot breathe for the weight of this, something caught in my own chest which somehow asks, "Mom, what happened that day Dad died? Who found him, did you?"

Our eyes just touch before she goes to sit, "Oh, yes, it was me that found him—here in our bed, asleep I thought at first, yet somehow I knew." She takes a breath as the scene begins, "He'd come home from golfing with his buddies saying that his arm was hurting. He started golfing several times a week since the mill retired him." Her eyes look distant as she talks, like she's watching all this on a television screen somewhere. "I called to him, touched his arm, and he felt cold lying there. God I was scared, so I called Darlene and she called the emergency squad. They got here quick. His friend Brownie was with them. He's the one came down-stairs to tell me, 'Jeanny,' he said, 'there's nothing more we can do—' I remember him standing right here where you are, saying that. 'There's nothing more we can do,'" and she sighs. "Brownie's a good old boy, been your father's friend since they were school boys."

"Was there a doctor who came?" I have to ask.

"No, just the paramedics, but then they took him straight to the hospital where he was pronounced dead." Suddenly she looks at me as though she has awakened out of a trance and is waiting for me to explain.

Only I can't. All I can say is, "It must have been hard for you. I'm sorry I wasn't around." There is a silence between us so still that we notice the hoot and crash of the mill as the trains take a haul of slag down to the pits. The mill is always there in this town—in the sounds and smells, the color of the air and in the talk—"What they got you workin', midnight?" "We'd come up, but Michael's workin' four-to-twelve next month...." Work is the fabric of life here.

Married at eighteen, my father worked as a brakeman on the railroad at Weirton Steel for forty years, till they forced him to retire. All this is *there* inside the room—his awareness of a life

"How'd you get through it all, Mom?"

"Well, Darlene was here, and your sister Debbie had come down by then. I think Dr. Ruksha came by and gave me something. I can't remember now. Debbie would."

There's another long silence as we think about all that's just been said. This is further than we've ever gone into it, the gritty details of a death, and it's almost as though we've stirred up a part of ourselves we thought was dead. I smile at her, "How come we never talked about this, Mom?"

She looks back, "I don't know." And then she thinks to say, "I know he's gone—Lord how I miss that old boy— but he's still here inside this house. You know, I can feel him sometimes. I think I hear him calling up from the basement, 'Honey, where's my work clothes?' or some such thing. I almost answer him, then I stop." She smiles quietly, "I guess I'm losing touch. But you know, I always feel better when I think of him, like having him back in a dream." I go over and hug her in her chair, and we can both sense the grief in each other. "What does it all mean?" she sighs, and I just hold her, so frail and quiet.

"You did all you could, Mom. All anyone can."

Now it is I who have to move about, so I walk out into the kitchen for a drink. The radio is playing the area talk show—"Will the schools be forced to consolidate if the mills don't pay back taxes?" It is a mix of local gossip and preparing for the worst. My wife's uncle Ron talks of retiring at forty-five. "What do I care?" he asks, "I can't let the mills decide my life. What's going to happen anyway, when it all shuts down? Have you thought of that?" And he shakes his head sitting on his front porch, "Who owns these mills? Who decides what happens here?" I shake my own head. "We steelmakers are a forgotten race," he concludes and I have no more answer for him than for my mother in the other room.

I could tell her of my own dreams of my father—of how he appeared in our house, smiling and tried to tell me a joke I couldn't get—how he laughed as if to say he was okay now. I know I felt good for a week, but dreams fade quicker than memories. Back in this valley the struggle toughens you or it breaks your heart. And where do you draw the line? I think of how my father didn't complain of his arm or chest on the day he died, and wonder if he might not be alive if he had. But, wasn't he trained here not to feel the pain, not to complain? Pouring my coffee, measuring my cream, I wonder how much we give up to survive? How much did my father?

I stir it together and I know these are futile questions, yet somewhere I've learned that ignoring a truth creates another sort of pain and a kind of blind numbness around the heart. I remember how Dad, scoutmaster of my youth, would stop our car on the street to breakup a kids' fight; he couldn't let a wrong go on. His working so hard, sending two boys through college, may have been his own way of rebelling against a silent lie. I take a drink of valley coffee and sit back down on the couch.

While my mother goes to take her medication I leaf through the local *Herald Star*. When she returns I ask, "Mom, what's this parade they're having uptown in Steubenville today—Festival Homecoming? Do you want to go?"

She smiles, "Sure, when is it?" Like a child now she welcomes small adventures and a chance for company. I know that kitchen radio is her best friend most days, that's why I bought it for her, and to quell my own guilt for moving away to my quiet home along the lake.

"They say at 2:00, but there's already a street fair on Fourth and Market if you want to take that in. Have you seen it?"

"Debbie and Michael took Robin the other night," as she sits. "They said she rode a pony in the street. I can't imagine that. A pony in the middle of Market Street that used to be so busy with traffic."

"Yeah," I say, and we both know the story of how the old downtown of Steubenville died four years ago after the layoffs, then again with the opening of the Fort Steuben Shopping Mall. And we both secretly wish we could be wrong about this, that the town will yet survive. Somehow our valley toughness doesn't exclude a capacity to dream.

At noon I show up again having retrieved my wife, son and daughter. My mother-in-law Sue has joined us in this summer thirst for a celebration. A widow like Mom,

Sue carries her John with her all the time. Instead of wearing a widow's black, she refused to smile for a year and a half. She's a strong Italian woman whose fierce integrity and hard work make her a legend in her neighborhood. John too did his 40 years in the mills, as a millwright—humble and happy on his job till they took it from him claiming his eyes were too weak. They were weak but twice as strong as the benefits the mill paid for his "early out." And while I know these forced retirements didn't kill our dads, I curse the thoughtless pain they brought to good people. Sue works now in the school cafeteria—baking cookies and cakes, fish and french fries for troops of teenagers. They give her a hard time but love her cooking. They always ask whether she cooked it before they buy...she is seventy.

My wife Ann and daughter Suzanne are like her in their strong will. In the Valley you learn early, if you learn at all, that work and self-belief are your strongest tools. My mother-in-law's favorite saying, besides "The rich get richer, and the poor get poorer" and "At least we eat good," is..."Well, we have each other."

Ann offers the front seat to my mother, but she refuses, climbing into the back—"No, no, we belong back here. Don't we, Sue? The merry widows and Suzanne." We all laugh, as Ann and Brian squeeze together; they begin to talk as I cruise up river to the celebration, to the hope a parade brings.

As we enter town from the North I search for a parking place—up close and free. I must prove to all these women that they haven't a fool for a son, husband or father. Finally, we pull onto the hot asphalt of the city lot, and I feed dimes to the meter. We cross the light down Adams to the street fair. The parade will follow these outside streets and march a square around the intersection of Fourth and Market. It's a good thing too, as those two streets are packed with noisy citizens barking back at the game keepers, standing in line for rides, or wolfing down Italian sausage and onions with a sudsy Budweiser in the afternoon. The whole street smells like a local bar, and there is hardly room to pass as we bump good naturedly into our neighbors. A flow in this human river, pushed on, I almost lose my wife who waves a hand above the heads. We laugh on the street corner, "So many people," I say, and she adds, "And we actually know some of them," an inside joke to small-town emigrants living in anonymous suburbs where the faces seem familiar yet you know none of them.

As a rock band blasts and rumbles from the flatbed of a truck, we feel at "home." And though we know this busy downtown street will become a deserted crime area again come Monday, for a while, our memory is washed by the flood of our senses.

Sue tells Ann to tell me that it's time to find a place to watch the parade, and so I look around then lead us back from Washington Street, only this time along the sidewalk, past the back of the Italian and Irish booths smelling of spaghetti and corned beef with nearly matching flags, past the abandoned J. C. Penney's building, the closed furniture and clothing stores—so empty and full of darkness—past the Slovak church's pirogue and raffle booth, to the corner of Fourth and Adams.

The old Capital Theatre has been leveled to build a store to sell tires and auto parts. It's been gone for years, but each time it hits me with its large sense of absence. In fact I realize that I have been vibrating with this same sense of presence and absence since we arrived. Struck by the sense of what is here and what is not, I struggle to assimilate the change.

In the midst of parents pushing their children toward a noisy, street merry-go-round, I recall how my wife and I once sat close together in the cushioned seats of the Capital Theatre while Tony and Maria of *West Side Story* sang so desperately of their love struggle. It was the first time we kissed. Perhaps my whole little family really began in search of such close moments? Perhaps. What I do know is that things change, even in this old town. Facing that, I know my real problem is understanding the direction of that change.

Waiting here on the curb along the corner, I've been noticing things. Not just the noise and vacant stores but the changed sense of the place. What has survived and how? The angry fumes of the One-Hour Dry Cleaners still spill out onto the street, and I remember its sickening smell and sticky feel as I picked up a suit standing there forced to breathe it as I watched the weary movement of the women at their mangles, caught the hurried tone of the clerks. And of course the bars are still here, one for every third storefront, and the Sports & Cigar places not driven out by the legal lottery. One bakery is still open, reminding me of time spent waiting for the bus breathing the hearty bread and donut smells till I had to purchase "Just one, please," from the Downtown Bakery. All the Five and Dime stores have been converted to self-serve drugstores, the restaurants to offices or video rentals, the clothing stores empty as night.

I stand there making this mental documentary when my daughter insists, "Dad, I'm hungry." We adults suddenly look to each other and realize she is right, we have forgotten lunch. I look back to the booths, then back at my son who is pointing down Adams Street; we smile, one of the brightest moments of the day, for we are a half block away from one of the best pizza shops in Ohio, perhaps the world.

"I'll be back in a minute," I tell them, and take my daughter's hand and follow Brian down the street to DiCarlos Italian Pizza. Inside, the mixed aromas of Parmesan cheese, warm dough, spicy pepperoni and sauce bring me back. It is a Roman pizza they make, sold by the square, and the crust is crisp yet chewy with juicy chunks of tomato melting into the mozzarella cheese and pepperoni which they throw on last like scattered seed. I point this out to my child, all the while remembering those years of standing at this same counter watching the rich ritual of the men tossing dough hard on counters, of their moving the pizza up the oven drawers as it rose steadily to a climax, cut and boxed, a rubber band snapped around the corners, the holes popped to keep it crisp. We buy two dozen and hurry back to our crowd, to that first bite into the steaming slab, chewing it well, a piece at a time. And it's good to taste how some things stay the same.

Standing as we eat, I notice the need for napkins, to catch the dripping but also to keep it clean from all the street dirt blowing along the curb. "It's a shame," Sue clucks, nodding to the way litter lies along the street—not just cigarette butts, though there are plenty of those, but whole bags from Burger King, empty pop and beer cans that the residents step over, like hard stones on the sidewalk. "The city levy didn't pass," I am told, and I nod as if I understand, but it is all wrong. Like watching your child pulled from a sports game, I am really torn that what seems so precious to me feels so easily abused. Yet I check my sense of righteousness knowing how much I've moved away from here, to my suburban life, a college teaching job, a safe haven along Lake Erie. I do not wish to accent my estrangement. I eat my pizza with my son on the curb.

People begin lining the curbs standing or seated in their lawn chairs. They stand and talk or occasionally watch up the street for the start of things. The police walk by us, a kid waits then darts across the street. Something is about to begin. Watching the faces of people standing near me I look for the familiar but find only the strange...a woman in a POISON T-shirt yanking her child up by the arm smacking her really hard on the butt, screaming "I told you to pee before we left!" this time with a smack to the face, "Didn't I?" No one says anything. "Well, didn't I?" The child only wails while the mother bellows, "Now, you run home, Missy, and change those pants. You'll miss the parade." The straw haired woman seems oblivious to all around her, as though the street is her home. This is something our parents and neighbors never did, no dirty laundry aired in the street. Her husband joins her now on stage and, yes, he is a hairy guy with those dark blue tattoos flaming up and down his arms. He brushes by her. "Hey, Babe, I'm goin' for a beer!" falls off his lips like spit, as he pushes his way through the crowd. "Oh, no you're not!" she shouts at him. "You're not leaving me here with these kids!" And it seems her whole life is a series of exclamations as she walks off leaving her children at our feet. They don't seem to notice, and most of the crowd looks back up the street trained now at ignoring these small unforgivable scenes of communal violence.

It is my mother-in-law who hisses, *"Sceevo"* and folds her pizza away in her napkin. It's an Italian expression, a succinct verb that means, "It makes me sick," and I know it is not the pizza but the mean ugliness that has repulsed her. It haunts the streets as I look hard at the faces in the crowd of locals who seem as strangely foreign to me as the news from Iraq. It's like watching the films made in this area—Michael Cimino's *The Deer Hunter*, or Peter Strauss' *Hearts of Steel*. The setting is right but the people are all wrong—not because they are actors but because they are portraying the valley and its people at their most desperate to preach Hollywood despair or false hope. That film life feels close yet alien to anyone who knows this place, a twin hurt that confuses me like these wounded faces around me. They are not the faces I grew up with here, those who lived well though poor and somehow shared the good that they had and were.

As I watch this woman turn back, I try to feel her life, guess her age, but it is impossible—the facial lines and cold eyes, the young children at our feet. She turns to us, motions to her kids, yells to my puzzled mother, "I'll be right back!" And so we find ourselves baby-sitting her girls on the street comer. The children take no notice until we offer them a pizza which they grab and gobble down, thanking us with their eyes. It's a sad scene, and this human gesture seems the only way to dispel the curse of this family's life. I need to understand.

"Mom," I turn to ask her, "Do you know these people?"

"Oh, no, I don't know her," she says, then realizes what I've asked. "There's a new crowd that lives downtown now."

"Where did they come from?" I hear myself ask.

She answers, "When everyone started moving out of downtown, they started moving in." She gestures broadly to the old buildings across the street, and I see above the storefronts, the backs of buildings, windows with ragged curtains, bags of trash out in the street beside junked cars. And my heart sags like the dirty clouds or this child's heavy diaper.

Sue adds, "Apartments are cheap now, because nobody wants to live where so many muggings go on." She goes on to report the worst and most recent incidents while I wonder which came first—the crime or the abandonment. She can't help telling these stories, because it has happened to her friends; it's a part of her life now. She plays out her old storyteller's hand—hoping by telling to somehow understand.

And I think of another conversation last week with a city planner now working as a car salesman. "No jobs for city planners," he jokes. So when I tell him of my dismay at understanding the way cities change, he describes for me the 'myth of urban renewal.' "See, they throw up a few new office buildings and a mall that look good to the outsiders. Right?" I remember nodding. "Only what you don't see is also what you get. To the city poor it means something else—less and worse housing. Where do you think all the 'homeless' people come from?" he asks while downing a half cup of coffee. "I'll tell you. Urban renewal drives some of them into the street and it drives a lot of others away to smaller cities like your hometown where they have no support, no sense of past, and no hope of a future. And so there they live unconnected, and just using up the present."

I had nothing more to say to him then or now to myself as this parade begins. I just stand here thinking: of the fathers who worked this valley farming labor into families along the river land, and of the widows now forced to watch the rich soil used up, spoiled by greed and unconcern. I know that my father had no answer for this either, and for once I am glad he doesn't have to be here to watch it all happen. I just stare across the street at an older man tending cars in the parking lot. He moves aimlessly from car to car, checking tags, and I recognize something in his face. My mother whispers his name, a classmate of mine, his face a shadow of my own.

Held there on the curb of the Steubenville street that feels so close yet strange, I become my own mute statue. I have no answers.

As the parade goes by, I watch how the faces light up at so little. The children are smiling at a clown squirting water from his motorcycle. A float of Junior Women toss candy at our feet. My mother waves to friends. I find myself nodding to everyone, yet inside myself I am thinking of the five words given to me by my ex-city planner: "Abandonment creates its own culture." It sums up my own confused pain now, and I say it over and over to myself, "Abandonment creates its own culture." In the summer heat, the parade passes, we smile into late afternoon sun, and then we take the widows home.

*   *   *

This essay strikes a chord of ambivalence toward home place yet captures for me, and I trust for many others, that struggle to recognize and understand the pain that accompanies change, especially when it is forced upon you and your community. This thoughtless abandonment of people and place is so pronounced in American culture where an arbitrary and unfeeling economy rules. I tried to put this here in human terms. As fellow writer Scott Russell Sanders had taught me, "You don't have to write from knowing. Just admit your confusion and write toward understanding." I've come to see how the town is still full of good people who help each other and care for family, their homes, and community.

Chapter Eight: The Family Expands/ Retirement

Much of the Smith family traveling shifted to our oldest daughter, Laura. Around 1989 she had just graduated from college with a degree in communication and with hopes for a job, so we had bought with her a small Ford Fiesta. The journalism job never happened because Laura couldn't stand the idea of spending her life working in an office, and so she and a college friend, Richelle, along with her wiry mutt, asserted their independence by deciding to launch a journey around the country searching for the best place to live and work. It took her to Bar Harbor, Maine; San Francisco, California; Boulder, Colorado; Taiwan (teaching English and following a guy); then to Portland, Oregon; Seattle and finally Bellingham, Washington. Often during those early years we would not hear from her for weeks and so learned that hard parents' role of letting go of control, though we couldn't stop worrying. Admittedly I envied her some of the adventures she was making, but we didn't know the cost it might be taking and so we lost sleep questioning her safety. Around this time I developed a fear of heights and driving over bridges. For me I had that same sense of being forced to trust the unknown. For Laura it was a time of facing challenges, finding beauty and friendship, and a new career in Portland where she worked as a waitress while training as a massage therapist. It's where she also met her future husband the author Allen Frost working alongside of her as a dish washer in Café Lena. Some 20 years later they have a daughter, Rosa, in college and a son Rustle in junior high. Their living out west has meant most of our travels have been to Bellingham to be with them and their flying back to their Ohio family.

Son Brian and his wife Anna stayed closer to home, both of them working with developmentally delayed adults in institutions and homes. With his degree in psychology, he walked into this low paying work easily, calling me early on to announce, "Congratulate me, Dad. I have my degree and now get to enjoy being working-class." After a few years in Columbus, they returned to Huron where Brian eventually decided to pursue a law degree at Akron University. It was a right career choice, and his native intelligence and hard work had him graduating at the top of his class. We sat with Anna and his young son, Adam, in the balcony watching as Brian graduated with honors. He has gone on to work as a labor lawyer on the side of the union workers. He and Anna divorced soon after a second son Alex was born, and yet the family has remained close.

Suzanne, eight years younger than Laura, took her path south to Ohio University near where the Smith family originated. There she excelled in psychology, gaining her bachelor's, master's and doctorate degrees in clinical psychology. She also met her tall husband, Joe Austerman while living in student housing in Ohio University's first coed dorm. While living with eight others in an off-campus house, Suzanne's abilities to organize things and coordinate people were tested, but she succeeded in helping the group at surviving and thriving. When she and Joe married, he in a Doctor of Ostepathic Medicine, she in clinical psychology, they found themselves wed yet living apart for a year to complete their internship studies. For a time they lived in Middle-town where Joe was raised. In 2002 they moved closer to us at University Heights in Cleveland and finally to a nearby suburb of Avon Lake. Daughter Maya was followed three years later by Alyssa and three years more by son Dylan. Suzanne served the Veterans at Wade Park for 11 years as a psychologist, then moved into private practice where she specializes in helping women and families through difficult challenges. Joe works with troubled youth at the Cleveland Clinic as a child and adolescent psychiatrist. The ideas of service and family came natural to both of them. With the birth of Zoe Miranda Smith to Brian and then partner Dawn Shaw, then Dylan to Suzanne and Joe, we now have eight unique and special grandchildren to care for and share our lives.

*　　*　　*

Soon cancer became the unwanted focus of my life causing anxiety and great questioning which ultimately yielded deep insights. Mine was discovered in 1998 after orthopedic surgeon and friend Rick Dwight urged me to have a prostate exam and PSA blood test. An ultrasound revealed two cancer shadows. Ann was wonderfully there for me as were my adult children each of whom I called to tell through tears, "Hello, this is Dad, I have cancer." When you hear those words, it immediately sounds like a verdict and a sentence, but then you discover the options for treatment ...watchful waiting, surgery, radiation, or a newer treatment by radiation seed implants...you begin to see a light. Unfortunately my urologist, who delivered the news to me over the phone before he took off for a week's vacation, did not mention any option other than surgery. We quickly checked its side effects—nerve damage, erectile dysfunc-tion, incontinence. The cancer was not advanced, yet everyone advised immediate treatment. After Ann and I did much research and sat with it in thoughtful talk, I chose with her approval the radiation seed implants being done at the Swedish Medical Center in Seattle, one of the best cancer treatment centers in the nation.

I flew out alone for pretesting and found what I had hoped for—caring attention and mindful assurances. They knew what I was going through personally, not just clinically. I began to imagine the life of a survivor. Later that day I recall sitting alone in a nearby coffee shop and reading that poet Denise Levertov, whom I so admired had just passed away from cancer there in Seattle. I remembered meeting her and her lovely voice and face as she read her pointed poems touching the truths of our lives. A favorite poem seemed now to portend her passing and thoughts of my own: "What Harbinger? A boat is moving/ toward me/ slowly but who/ is rowing and what/ it brings I can't/ yet see."

Levertov delivers such delicate yet brave writing. Once at the James Wright Poetry Festival in Ohio, I had confessed to her my admiration, and she had embraced me. Sitting in the soft café light, I found I could not finish my coffee. Only later did I learn that her death came at the same Swedish Medical Center which I had just come from. Her life was ended or passed beyond this world, mine had begun again with good care and hope.

A month later I returned with Ann for the outpatient procedure. We checked into the quiet Seattle hotel connected with the hospital, and after a brief pre-op exam, the procedure was done with me as an outpatient, lying on a surgery table under anesthesia and vaguely hearing the targeting of my prostate. That night and the next day I was to watch my urination for any of the hundred rice shaped seeds that might have come loose. Happily I found none, and once the catheter and bag were removed the next day, I was released with the only warning, "For a few days, you may feel as though you had sat upon a cactus."

Before we left town, Ann and I were able to walk the downtown streets of Seattle where I was strangely drawn to a corner shop that sold gems and stones. There I bought a small incense holder made of soap stone, the stone of cancer. All that month I had been turning away from the common practice of "fighting" or "battling" cancer to an image of befriending it and so turning away its power by saving my energy for healing. This homeopathic approach, though not as common as the allopathic, was hard to explain to others, even family. It did not mean giving in to cancer or surrendering, but rather learning from it and finding the most comfortable, livable stance toward it, then doing a kind of ju-jitsu on its power to destroy and so welcome real healing of both body and spirit. It did not remove the cancer, but gave it meaning in my life.

What You Realize when Cancer Comes

You will not live forever—
No, you will not, for a ceiling of clouds hovers in the
    sky.
You are not as brave as you once thought.
Words of death echo in your breast.
You feel the bite of pain, the taste of it running
    through your veins.
Following the telling to friends comes a silence of
    felt goodbyes.
You come to know the welling of tears.

Your children are stronger than you thought and
    closer to your skin.

. . . .

You are in a river, flowing in and through you.
    Take a breath. Reach out your arms.
        You can survive.
A river is flowing, flowing in and through you.
    Take a breath. Reach out your arms.
        You can survive.

I remember sharing this poem with the men's cancer support group to which I belonged. They deeply appreciated it, and I them as fellow survivors. But when asked to share the poem with the general public at a Relay for Life gathering, the audience seemed not ready for its hard truths. Though the ending rises to survival, I suppose the poem's directness was too much for them, and I was not asked back, but these poems have been shared among many persons and families dealing with cancer.

Entering retirement at 65 meant release, but it was also a painful letting go of what had been so central to my life. I had to resist the advice of many others..."Oh, don't stop working." "Now you can move south." "You are going to regret it." And so I soon learned that the best advice is no advice. Each must find his or her way. Yet I could record the stages of the experience for me, as I did in this poem:

Clearing Out My Office

No, I've not been fired or let go.
I'm releasing myself after 42 years
of teaching at this college.
Letting go of a career as it were,
using past tense now for the first time.

And I stand alone in this small room
deciding what to save, what to give away,
what to throw in the trash.
Book after book, folder after folder,
knowing I will never teach this again,
yet feeling its weight in memory, in value
given and received from the reading
and conceiving, the sharing together,
the way it can happen in the classroom.
Thousands of faces come streaming back:
some of them eager, some questioning,
some resisting or hardly awake,
all to be opened to the possible.

I've made stacks for the books:
some for the Free Books out in the hall,

some for the library, some special for colleagues,
some for Good Will, and some so riddled with notes
I think to drop them in the trash, but can't.
They stick in my hands like projects in wood
I've made or carved over the years.
I have always loved books...seen as roadways,
or life-savers and ropes to pull one to safety
or out beyond yourself.
I pile the cups and pens and photos
into a box and set it out in the hall,
turn off the computer screen and the light.
I take a breath and close my eyes,
then lug boxes out to the car.

This letting go, a necessary hurt,
is a pain to pass through like birth.
Walking to the car, I smile, knowing that
for all of these years I've been paid
for doing what I love.

With more time available after retirement in 2003, I sought to find my place and purpose for this new phase of life. At first I trained as a hospice volunteer and did that work for two years aiding the elderly like my grandmother and providing respite care by sitting with those who were dying. There were life lessons in small pockets of experience, feeding a woman with dementia, chatting with her table of friends, being with a woman who reached 100 with the simple request, "Let me die." Then I trained as a volunteer for CASA (Court Appointed Special Advocate), a job that proved vital yet really difficult. Though I was to represent the child for the magistrate, yet most often my dealing was with the disputing divorced parents and with a broken system of social services whose prosecutor's office too often dealt with things by dividing family members and generally enacting threats and punishments. I found so much judgment upon the families from the social services officers that I often became the only one the family trusted and with whom they would communicate. Lawyers proved disappointing, typically talking badly about their own clients in private session. Ultimately I resigned after two years when I felt pressure from CASA administers to accept and support the prosecutor's views in what should have been an independent advocacy. I was beginning to see that retirement was no easy task. My only advice to new retirees has been to take no advice. It's a path you must make.

*   *   *

Though foreign travel did not often fit our budget, in later years Ann and I did manage a tour of France, and another of Scotland and Ireland with my brother David and his wife Joan. If Italy had moved Ann with a sense of life connection, Scotland did that for me. Besides the Scot wit, I recognized in the land where my Great Grandfather Alexander Cochran had originated a deep sense of connection. The village of Alloway where poet Robert Burns had lived felt much like the Appalachian foothills were my family had thrived. My grandmother Putnam had passed on to me through my mother a book of Burns' poetry which had come down from her own Scot father. Standing at the famous and lovely Brig 'o Doon bridge watching sheep rest along its lush green banks, I know that David and I shared a quiet sense that we had come home to a beautiful place. But we also recognized that, like so many others, our Scot-Irish ancestors had labored hard and long in the mines there and had come to America for a chance at a better life.

Spiritual travels also played out in our lives for Ann and me, though often we experienced them separately. At least half a dozen summers I had travelled to Concord, Massachusetts, home of Transcendentalists Ralph Waldo Emerson, Henry David Thoreau, Louisa Mae Alcott, Nathaniel Hawthorne, and others. At times I took students there on summer fieldtrips. But chiefly I enjoyed staying near and walking Walden Pond alone at dawn and dusk (with Thoreau at my side). Woodstock and Mt. Tremper, New York, in the Adirondacks became a Buddhist destination several times where I found instruction and deep connections at the Zen Mountain Monastery. Ann's travels took her to rustic Pumpkin Hollow retreat center, near Rhinebeck, New York, where she developed a practice of Therapeutic Touch, learning from mentors who worked to heal others through their sensing of energy through chakras. I've watched and felt this happen. Related to this, Ann trained to become a Reiki master at The Pines in nearby Fremont. She now has her own practice in a home office space. Ann has also trained for years with the Sacred Art of Living and Dying group which fosters caring for the dying and their families.

Together we did some training on meditation and mindfulness with Thich Nhat Hanh at his Blue Cliff Mountain Retreat Center and with Tara Brach at Kripalu in Stockbridge, Massachusetts. All of this has resulted in our co-founding with friends Jan and Lou Young the Converging Paths Meditation Center in Sandusky, Ohio. As we say, "It is an open and safe space to meditate with others." Humble and tied to no religion but open to all, on a weekly basis, it is where for nine years now much of our spiritual growth and service takes place. The journey inward is endless.

Increasingly we were and are part of a church community. In this case St. Peter's Catholic Church in downtown Huron. Though our children would go to public schools, they also took religion classes at St. Peter's where we attended regularly. Ann as a Catholic all her life, me as a "sitting catholic" who for decades came to church with my young family and eventually kneeled with them.

Together with Ann we discussed the sermons or homily, but I did not join the church. Perhaps something of my Protestant rearing prevented it. Though many of our friends were reared as Catholic, most seemed to have moved away from the Church due to bad experiences or splits over some of its moralistic stands against homosexuality, divorce, and abortion. I knew I was standing near a spiritual center though not embracing it.

When we would visit home in Mingo, I would go to "church" with my parents discovering over the years an ever-shrinking congregation of Presbyterians. In fact my deeper connection remains toward a contemplative practice with its very openness and acceptance to all. However, for decades I could not commit to being a Buddhist anymore than I could being a Catholic. My self-identity was too independent, and I couldn't resolve some inner conflicts. At this stage in my life I saw myself (as one writer puts it) as "buddish" and lower case christian. I found companionship and comfort in the broader earth-life writings of Wendell Berry. In his "The Peace of Wild Things" he answers life's noise and struggle with this:

> I go and lie down where the wood drake
> rests in his beauty on the water,
> and the great heron feeds.
> . . . .
> I come into the presence of still water.
> And I feel above me the day-blind stars
> waiting for their light. For a time
> I rest in the grace of the world, and am free.

In such writing and visions I feel myself grounded in the natural world. Here Thoreau and Buddha and Christ welcome each other. This pervasive light, "the grace of the world," whatever its source, becomes the felt truth behind my life and writing. Another quote linked it to people. "In the grace of simple people/ we all learn to survive." I was back where I began because I had never left the path of finding compassion and truth in self and others.

Increasingly I began to sense my life as made up of intersecting planes. Existing in time and in place, but also in social and spiritual contexts, they manifest in realms of inner awareness. Within me was my working-class youth, my nuclear and extended family, my work and growth experience with others, my awareness of spiritual pathways and great movements in art and writing—all of it and more inside of me. These planes of being formed my own storied world, the one that I was and am writing here. Despite this diversity, or maybe because of it, I was a larger whole. "I am what I am," cry Moses and Christ and Popeye. At 70 I joined the Catholic Church and feel at home enough to volunteer as a reader at Mass and as a part of the charitable St. Vincent de Paul Society. At the heart of my writing has always been the need to explore my own converging paths, to sense their passages and see their interconnection: in essence, to share this sense of life with and for others in my deeds and in my writing which we turn to now.

Town and Family Photos

Mingo Junction with Wheeling-Pitt Steel Mill

Smith Family 1943
Standing: Carrie, holding David, Harry, Ernie, Murray and wife,
Monte; Kneeling: Jean (pregnant with Larry), Mary;
with Martha Ray, Sonny, and their mother Boots

Mother, Jean Smith, Jean Putnam,
Delbert with Raymond Putnam
and David and Larry c.1946

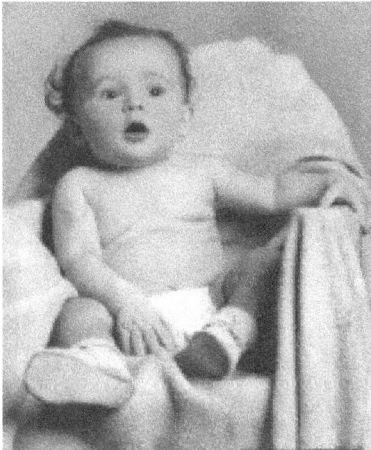

Baby Larry (1943)

Uncle Harry "Satch," home for WW II,
grandparents Carrie and Ernie Smith
(1945, year Ernie is killed on the railroad)

View of Wheeling-Pitt blast furnace from school windows

Jean Smith before Larry's birthplace

Home at 310 Murdock Street

Mingo Junction (photo by James Jeffrey Higgens)

Larry c. 1949

Janis, Larry, and David c. 1952

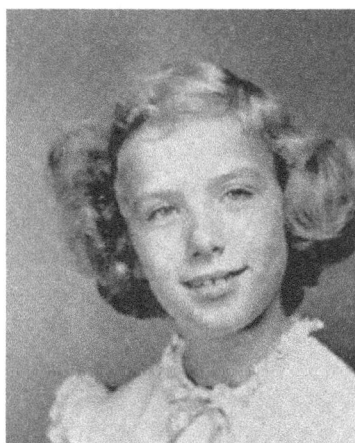

Larry   Classmates   Shirley Mae c. 1954

Larry in suburban coat with sister Debbie, c. 1956

Class of 1961 Mingo Central High School

Class of 1961 Mingo Central High School, Note key figures marked
with dot: Shirley, Barbara, Kenny, and Larry

Two Worlds

Muskingum College, Brown Chapel

Weirton Steel blast furnace area where Larry
worked summers of 1964 and 1965

Ann Zaben, graduation photo
Wheeling School of Nursing, 1965

Larry graduation photo
Muskingum College, 1965

Wedding at St. Agnes Catholic Church, Mingo Junction,
July 3, 1965 John Zaben, Ann and Larry Smith, Father Bellfield

Euclid Senior High School where Larry taught 1965-1968

Ann with baby Laura,
Euclid, Ohio 1967

Larry with baby Laura,
Blisswood Home, Euclid, 1967

Sue & John Zaben with grandchildren:
Brian, Suzanne, and Laura, 1976

Deb and Jean Smith with grandson Brian, and Larry, 1977

Smith family in Sicily, Ann, Suzanne, Laura,
Brian, Larry, 1981

Larry and Ann on bridge in Florence, Italy 1981

Firelands College of Bowling Green State University, Huron, Ohio

Larry Smith

Larry teaching at Firelands College, 1970-2010

Bill Wright (91) and Larry at "Occupy Sandusky" rally, 2011

Larry with "The Boys," grandsons Adam and Alex Smith, 2013 and below, 2016

The arc of the lake
sweet scent of grass and trees
cricket song to the wild
a step at a time
inside the rim

Old Woman Creek Estuary in Huron, Photo by Brian, Poem by Larry

Ann and Larry in backyard in Huron, 2015

Smith family c. 1997 Laura, Allen, baby Rosa, Larry, Suzanne,
Ann, Brian, Anna

Smith family, 2014 Standing: Brian, Adam, Alex, Suzanne, Joe,
Maya, Allen, Rosa, Laura, Rustle; Seated: Zoe, Ann, Dylan, Larry,
Pokey (dog), Alyssa (photo by Brian Smith)

Part Two

River of Stones: My Writing Life

"In the most general way, writing is about soul making for one individual writer, but I believe it can also be about making the soul of the world. Not to sound too high-minded about it, but writing can make a difference in the world around us."
— Sue Monk Kidd

Photo by Brian Smith

Sense how
Even the smooth stones ache
With stories of their own
In the shuddering light of day.
— Scott Hastie

Chapter Nine: Early Writings of Home
& Imaginative Release

Am I a teacher who writes or am I a writer who teaches? Am I a working or middle class person? Am I a poet, fiction writer, essayist, biographer or film writer? Am I a trained scholar or a popular reviewer? Am I a literary author or a populist writer? What begs to be asked of all of these questions is—Can I be both or all? I've faced all of these questions by taking on the roles of each, trying on the clothes of each and finding what fits, ultimately seeing myself as the many in one. Perhaps my writing life goes back to that sixth grade classroom of Mrs. Merzi and those poem booklets she handed out to us expecting us to read and write from them. Yet I know that I have always loved language and making things with words even as a child. While my writing is not my life, it is essential to it and provides its landmarks. As poet Gary Snyder suggests, our writing work becomes a riprap of stones marking a life path and revealing its levels and pathway to true self. In a somewhat rare way (though not for writers) I have my writing as a separate map into my life. My love of language thus forms the first broad stone as a basis for the others. As a means of further understanding and sharing the dynamics of my life and work, I mark here my writer's passageway.

My first publications did not come until the 1970s when I was in my twenties and writing in the early mornings or late evenings while also teaching writing at Firelands College and caring for family. Certainly I had written much before, but it typically was for academic studies or it ended in a letter home or in a desk drawer, not to be seen or heard from again and yet kept. However, following Gary Snyder's 1968 visit to Kent State and the tragic 1970 shootings there, and then my college teaching, I felt both increased confidence and the need to share. If reading great literature could save us, so the writing of it was part of engaging life. I recall my father asking me once as I sat reading on the back porch, "Why do you read so much? Don't you want to do things?" I looked up in dumb silence, then followed him into his basement work area, saying, "You know, Dad, some of my reading has saved my life. Like your reading the Bible, it helps me and others get through." He returned that look of silence, then nodded, "Okay. I hear you." And so it is not surprising that my early poems were firmly rooted in my Ohio Valley youth. One of the first came in *From These Hills*, a regional magazine, appearing alongside of writing by and about Earl Hammer, who wrote "The Waltons" television series. From the start I was connecting to my Appalachian home place and its people. The poem bore the simple title:

Ohio Valley Steel Town

Old store fronts
with new signs—
green screen doors boasting
of Wonder bread
and Ne-Hi pop.

Cars double park
in front of Islay's
while old men walk
under streetlights
stopping to bolt a shot
and bet the number
of his daughter's new house—
or some other dream of his.

Wives wait
in rough-sided houses

or vaults of new brick.
They sweep the soot
from porches
and sit on swings
quietly watching
for their men
climbing the hill
to them.

Their children have gone
to college or just
moved away,
leaving
memory ghosts of
real towns colored dark
by the sweat of living people.

Only the night Bessemer
celebrates in a burst
of pink-orange light
the river, the hills,
the town, the lives.

Not only was I asserting a self-identity here, but charting an identity for my town and its way of life. Portraits of town and people arrive in a collage of images with feelings. The influence of fellow Ohio poets James Wright and Kenneth Patchen can be felt in the directness of voice here and its attempt to capture the story of place. By 1975 these and other seasonal poems were published in my first book, *Growth: Poems and Sketches* from Northwoods Press.

As each book has a story, this one, though painful, ties to the publisher Robert Olmsted, who printed the first edition as he later admitted, "while in the bottle." After months of waiting, the books arrived on campus in a box that I opened excitedly in my office. Here at last I thought was my work in substance and form. As I pulled out a copy, my heart sank. I held in my shaking hands the most botched job of printing I've ever seen...pages awkwardly printed and out of alignment, spine already coming apart. Shame rather than pride overwhelmed me. I closed my office door. These mistakes were not because Olmsted didn't know how to do a book, but because he was an alcoholic drinking heavily at the time and so unable or unwilling to care. My sadness soon turned to anger. Days later after some threatening letters and phone calls, Olmsted did reprint the book in a decent format, so by the end of the month, I held them again. But I had learned something about setting hopes too high and risking vanity. Like any business or art, writing and publishing could be spoiled by neglect or greed.

The book sold well to family and friends and colleagues. Because so much of it is tied to family, my father's response threw me. He said simply, "It seems rather a sad book." I responded, "Oh, no, Dad. It's nostalgic, the sweet sadness of memory." I don't think he believed me, and maybe the book's opening poem suggests why.

A Way Out

> While the children of lives
> ache in the aisles of order
> school in the building of system
> break and mend again broken,
> grass grows on the lawns of hope.

When I spoke as a child
I was a child.
Now I put away peace
and live in the house of my father.
Now I sit on grey shores
of dread.

> I'd have written
> you sooner, but
> I learned the language
> at eight of non-
> communication.

Twenty years have only now
brought me to the verge
of
speech.

Though I now find this poem a bit affected and over-dramatized in its statement of alienation and rebellion, I also sense my honest reaching to express some common themes of youth. In *Growth* I felt the seeds of transformation. I had molded my life and my art into a statement and shared it hoping to reach a universal other. Though I had much to learn about my craft, this first book helped me to walk more comfortably as a person and a poet. The growth recorded in this book is measured out in spoons of truth discovered and in finding human expression. I had found my writer-self. When I meet new writers struggling with the question of whether they are truly writers, I always ask, "Are you writing?" If they nod in agreement, I reply, "Well, then you are a writer." Speaking for them and myself, I add, "Put away that self-doubt as a great block and silencer. Just do it. It matters." Later I would recommend that the writing must matter to you, to the work itself, and to the readers.

Imaginative Release

By 1974 when Richard Nixon was forced to resign his presidency over the Watergate fiasco, I had finished writing my long dissertation on Ohio writer, Kenneth Patchen and received my Ph.D. in contemporary literature. A photo from then at Kent State shows a bearded Larry with 2 year old Brian on his shoulder, daughter Laura and wife Ann at his side. We had made it as a family. And in the summer of 1976 I received a summer fellowship from the National Endowment of the Humanities. I was to study Surrealism with J. H. Matthews at the University of Syracuse. Our whole family, including baby Suzanne, traveled to Syracuse where we lived most of that summer in married student housing. The course was brilliant, as was Matthews, and I formed several alliances with other fellows, especially artist Stephen Smigocki. He and I would develop there an idea for collaboration. The result emerged in the imaginative book, *Echo Without Sound: Poems by Larry Smith and Etchings by Stephen Smigocki* (Northwood Press, 1982). An example is "Deliveries":

> A lunchbox suddenly dreams it's a hotel
> with rooms, restaurant, and a heated pool.
> It dreams itself awake.
> No one will touch it now. It's not what they expect.
> They wanted more. They wanted less.

("One passing overhead; then another one"
etching by Stephen Smigocki)

One can sense the influence of dream and automatic writing here where strangeness is matter of fact to the subconscious. Stephen's magical etchings hatched much the same way from automatic drawing would lie beside my poems in a further kind of happy connection, again from the subconscious. He and I laid the book out at my parents' home in Mingo Junction where we used their living room floor to set his prints with my poems. In defense of art, we had to lock my mom's cat in the closet. After hours of work, we shared beers on the back porch listening to the sounds of the birds and mill works.

h h h
t   t   t   t
w   w   w
o   o
r
g

Poems and Sketches

by LARRY R. SMITH

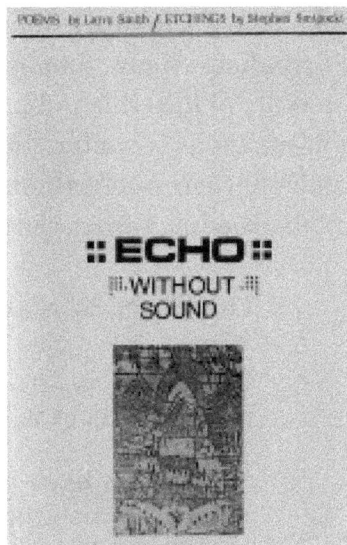

:: ECHO ::
WITHOUT
SOUND

POEMS by Larry Smith / ETCHINGS by Stephen Sedgwick

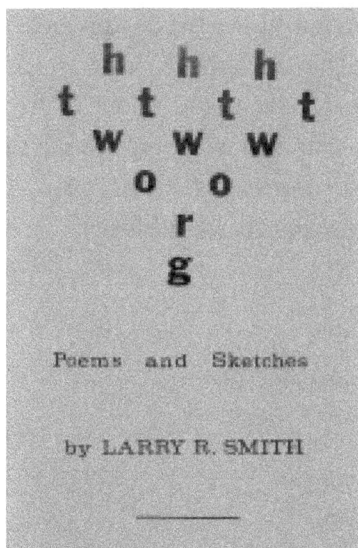

Growth: Poems and Sketches   *Echo Without Sound*
(1974)   (1982)

During the late summer of 1978, not wanting to neglect my own creative writing, I traveled to the famed Breadloaf Writers Conference in Vermont's rustic Green Mountains. Here I would learn from fellow writers such as Charles Simic, Mark Strand, Toni Morrison, and John Gardner in large group talks and readings, and in more private sessions. It was a friendly atmosphere, though there was a clear hierarchy of top writers, their assistants, and we common participants. Living close there that week allowed me to see writers as persons with their families and their own methods of writing and diverse styles of teaching. In Simic's writing workshop he reviewed my writings that were so heavily influenced by the illogical intuition of Surrealism. Though it fit with much of his own writing, his advice was, "Well, this is good, but no one will ever publish it." He was wrong on that score as Cleveland State University's Poetry Center soon published a chapbook of my poems and prose poems in *Scissors, Paper, Rock* (1978), my third book of poetry. I had been drawn to the deeply beautiful work of imaginative and intuitive American Surrealists Simic, James Tate, Russell Edson, and W. S. Merwin. While this publication did give a real boost to my self-image as a writer, the press was not well equipped to promote their publications, and so I found myself arranging public readings from that book of dreamlike fables.

The Story of Marriage

Trees grow in the space between us.
We touch them when we have time.

All day you have been turned
looking at the stones within.
And I have been watching you
like a fish.

Comes a time and you are watching me
digging holes in the sand.
And between us lies the sea
where the birds are thick with silence.

Then in the night falls a seed
beside us.
We pick it up together the next day.
It opens to the song of children laughing.

The sky falls each day, they say.
Only some days we catch it in our arms.

There is extreme trust in emotion and a subconscious sense of relationships here. This faith in intuitive communication seems to me now as a blend of Surrealism and Zen Buddhism. It feels as though a deeply intuitive voice is caught in the act of telling a dream, an old person speaking stories around a fire. Here is another in that vein:

An Old Story

There is the story of too much food.

Of the herds of women flocked around a fire plucking chickens and roasting hogs that the men throw on the ground before them. The men keep returning to the woods and barns bringing more. One woman skirts up her dress to carry the fresh carrots and potatoes, so many her rump is showing. Another with hair wrapped about her head fills white bowls that they bring in rough hands with quarts of black coffee. The bowls hang from their waists like the tails of cows. Everybody hums. Slabs of bread soaked in warm butter are passed around while the fresh slaughtered beef fill the ground with their blood.

And no one stops to talk or sit down.

There is no other work.

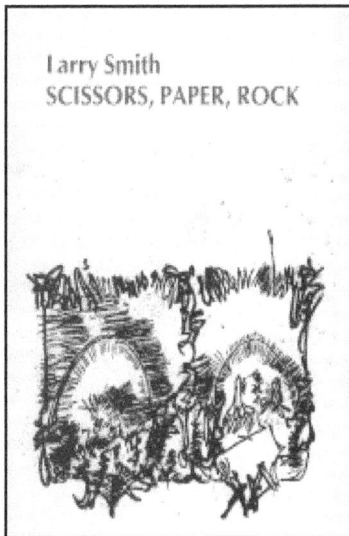

Larry Smith
SCISSORS, PAPER, ROCK

Scissors, Paper, Rock (1978)
(cover by Stephen Smogocki)

Author photo from 1978

The book reached a limited audience, yet it also introduced me to the director of the Cleveland Poetry Center, Alberta Turner. A remarkable woman, as a writer and friend she showed me how to trust what comes and as a teacher how to organize a group of writers into an open sharing center. The Firelands Writing Center emerged in 1979 as a cooperative of writers dedicated to publishing and promot-ing fine regional writing. Though I was still exploring and finding my voice, I had earned academic credentials and community validity as an Ohio writer. I only had to continue doing good work as life wrote upon me.

Chapter Ten: Author Appreciations
& The Birth of Bottom Dog Press

My book *Kenneth Patchen* (Twayne: U.S. Authors Series) on the daring writing and life of this Ohio author was published in 1978 as the first book on this renowned writer-artist. When my Kent State advisor, Sanford Marovitz, said, "Well, Larry, you are now the Patchen man," I had to think that over. Yes, I had done the research and created a broader appreciation for this neglected writer. Yes, I quickly knew more about him and his work than almost anyone else in the literary world, because I hadn't been stopped by his maverick stance toward the academic and publishing worlds nor by his subsequent critical neglect. A key revelation here was my personal focus on treating neglected work and artists, obviously a reflection of my own experience of struggling to be seen at Muskingum and Kent academia. With the completion of this book I again felt confirmed as a writer.

The book's manuscript had waited on Twayne's shelf with others for two years before I received it back with detailed instructions for edits to be done—within two weeks. I was angry at this treatment, yet so eager to see the book out that I stopped complaining and immediately set to making the suggested edits. The book champions Patchen's engaged, diverse, and dynamic writing. I loved quoting fellow writers who praised his work: "For a characterization of the Patchen stance and strength we turn to poet William Everson: 'I best see Patchen as one who cocks a terrible right arm against the glass jaw of New York, stunning it with all the contradiction of its values he can summon against it. . . . as the poet always survives the metropolis that hates and ignores him in the moment of his accusation. Bless him in his pain and passion, for his cry is heard.'" So well put is this statement of the shared defiance of the status quo, it speaks for me as well. Looking back now, I can see how my writing, like my life, had moved from models (Robert Frost, William Carlos Williams; even my brother in life) to perceived allies (Patchen, Snyder, Everson, Ferlinghetti). That year, to my own surprise, I was noted as the most published author in Bowling Green's English Department.

The year 1980-1981, was our Fulbright year abroad when we released home and friends to live in Sicily. At the University of Catania, Sicily, I taught a course in "American Romanticism and the Beat Movement" with professor Maria Victoria DiAmico. But as our family recalls, it was more a year of learning than teaching as we experienced a culture as well as a new language and land. As I tell elsewhere, it was an exciting and challenging time in which we struggled yet survived well as a family. Though I wrote a short collection of poems in Italy, they lacked the grounding in voice and place which I valued.

Once back in America I had something to attend to. Soon after we had arrived in Sicily, I met with my colleague Maria Vittoria DiAmico at her town apartment. It was all quite lovely until she handed me my mail and I discovered a rejection letter of a book biography which I had done on poet-publisher Lawrence Ferlinghetti. Gray Fox Press, who had agreed to do the book, now found my emphasis on detail and scholarship offsetting. I had read all of Ferlinghetti's books and interviewed him and other writers and friends for weeks in San Francisco. I had hung around old Beat café's and bookstores and gone over his manuscripts at his place. Ferlinghetti wanted the book done because he felt himself known for his City Lights Books as a publisher, but underappreciated as a writer of poetry, plays, and fiction. As he reminded me, his early *A Coney Island of the Mind* book of poems had sold almost a million copies. I agreed with him; he deserved fuller recognition and so my work had that intention. When I returned to America my literary biography was accepted immediately after my first query to Southern Illinois University Press. With a year abroad and a new book coming out I was again the outstanding scholar in the English department.

Kenneth Patchen (1978)

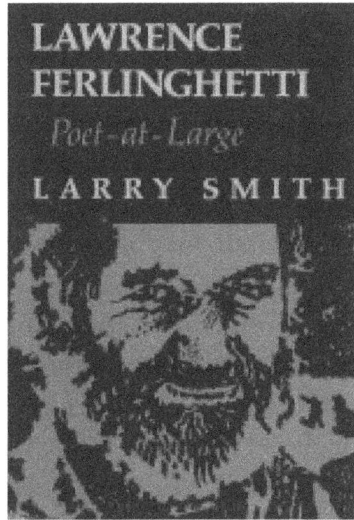

Lawrence Ferlinghetti:
Poet-at-Large (1982)

The Birth of Bottom Dog Press

In late 1984, following the heartfelt death of my father and then my railroad journey west to California, came the birth of Bottom Dog Press, a nonprofit organization dedicated to publishing deserving books of people and places. Fellow poet David Shevin and I founded it with the guidance of another colleague and mutual friend, Robert Fox. My *Across these States*, dedicated "In memory of Delbert R. Smith (1921—1984)/ My railroader father" was our first signed limited edition book published. I would have loved for my father to see and read this book, yet it remains a bond of caring between us. The press' origins can be traced to my research out west. For while in Berkeley scouring the shelves of the California authors and reading their work, I was also learning how small press publications could develop and evolve out of clear heartfelt intentions and a craft of making a book or magazine. Many such publications had short lives of a couple years because the writer-editor-publishers could not or would not work at keeping them solvent and sustaining. My work on writing and directing grants and the managing side of teaching had taught me some of these survival skills.

On a more practical level, it came about from the generosity of an older man, somewhat like my father. Joseph Curran arrived as an unusual looking angel at my office door one afternoon. He lived in nearby Vermilion, Ohio, and had heard of my work with the writers' group, the Firelands Writing Center. I soon learned of his role as a publisher of miniature books; in fact he was president of the American Independent Publishers Organization. He declared simply, "I've heard of your what you're doing and wonder if I might help in some way." He showed me some of his fine letter press books done on his basement printing press. Then we talked for more than an hour: me sharing my vision of one day publishing, he sharing practical advice about the process. He gave me his phone number and told me to call when I was ready. That weekend I called him back saying, "Yes. I'm ready."

Joseph mentored our first publication, coaching me on the process and costs. We drove together to Mansfield's Meade Paper Company to pick up enough cream colored, laid stock for the text printing and a flecked gray for the cover, all from their leftover stock. He was teaching me thrift as well as process. My artist friend Zita Sodeika (Willard, Ohio, by way of Chicago, by Lithuania) produced the line drawing for the cover, a block series of visions from a train engine. Joseph produced the text on a fine letterpress printer in his basement. When they were done, he called me to come and pick up the pages. On the drive over I realized that I had never talked price with Joseph, and that I had no idea what he would ask. I had a couple hundred in our personal checking account. Joseph took me down to the basement, showed me his marvelous printing machine, and then the pages of the book. They were laid out in stacks of 14, covering pages 1-28. Black Caslon type was stamped deep into the cream paper, enough for 300 copies...a couple extra in case of accidents. As he loaded the boxes into my arms, I dared to ask, "This is so wonderful. How much do I owe you, Mr. Curran?"

There was a slight pause till he responded, "You owe me nothing, my friend. I'm glad to do this, and maybe someday you'll do the same for someone else who's starting out." A handshake and another thank you, and I drove the book home where my family gathered round our dining room table like a train, collating the text of 300 books. Joseph had already taught me the process of scoring and stitching the books binding and handed me my own template and awl. We used good thick thread, tying a double knot in the center of the first fold, allowing the string to lay out a little. From these humble beginnings arose our dedication to paying it forward by publishing deserving writing that mattered to all people.

In *Across these States: Journal Poems* I had found my role as observer-recorder of life in the details. The forward movement of the train was balanced by sideward watching of the people and land:

> I wake to the window.
> Late evening and a red Mustang races
> beside the long train.

Piles of old railroad ties
burn beside the tracks as
night is passing us.
That fine light of dusk
makes everything tender and close.

Two girls in shorts race along
on bikes toward Galesburg,
gentle silhouettes in fading sun.
. . . .

Why do brakemen always talk
as though they just had a drink?
I hear my father's brakeman voice
in theirs, ripe work-talk
around a kitchen table,
railroad pulsing in the blood.

The darkness falls on the banks
where a young doe flashes
into the trees. It turns
to watch us pass.

It was an easy book to write in many ways as I only had to
stay awake to the life around me, and the loose journal form
allowed for witness and reflection in a casual voice. Early
on I reflect on the sound of a train ahead:

Outside the hills begin to roll
into red brick Indiana.
Almost asleep, a distant whistle—
lost crooning in the night—
it's from the train I'm on.

"Write the life around you" the journal form seemed to say,
and so I did.

Our second book at Bottom Dog Press came the following year as *36 Spokes: The Bicycle Poems*, another journal poem book, by poet and friend Terry Hermsen. In close detail it covered his and his wife's biking trail across America. I had loved books all of my life. Now I would work at making them with a press that today has survived for more than 30 years with 200 books.

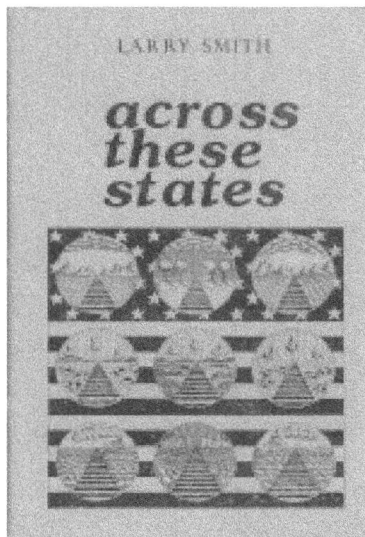

across these states (1985)   **36 Spokes (1986)**

The cover art for both books and many to come from Bottom Dog Press was by artist Zita Sodeika. The bottom dog title and logo, made by extracting the fangs from a wolf, suggest the feisty image and spirit of the underdog. The name comes from a book by Edward Dahlberg who wrote so well of working-class life. Our early marketing was through family and friends and fellow writers, and I eventually took the press to a bookfair in Canton, Ohio, where they held the annual Midwest Writers' Festival. Our table was alongside of Bob Fox's Carpenter Press. I remember getting a cup of coffee and walking back to see our small display of two books and just beaming with pride and disbelief that we could be a part of a literary scene and tradition. As a fellow writer and friend David Budbill has said in a poem "The Ubiquitous Day Lily of July" there is strength in the humble which stands forth with resilience and persistence.

> There is an orange day lily that blooms in July and is everywhere around these parts right now. Common. Ordinary. It grows in everybody's dooryard . . . .
> . . . it's coarse and ordinary and it's beautiful because it's ordinary. A plant gone wild and therefore become rugged, indestructible, indomitable, in short: tough,
>   resilient,
> like anyone or thing has to be in order to survive.

Larry sewing bindings on *Across these States,*
first Bottom Dog Press book (1985)

Bottom Dog Press

Chapter Elven: Native Zen and Voices

My next book *Ohio Zen Poems* would be a twin book of Zen nature and meditative poetry done with fellow Ohio poet d. steven conkle and published by Bottom Dog Press in 1989. Having read and practiced Zen Buddhism for some years, I decided to study it further at the Zen Mountain Monastery in Mt. Tremper, New York. Here John Daido Lorri had guided a group of American practitioners with an emphasis on Zen arts. During my brief stays, my poems found kindred spirits. I watched archers learn to cast arrows without aiming, cooks become one with their food, sitters let go of all to "just sit." I saw no issue then nor now with accepting Buddhism and a belief in a God which embraces finding the "true self." Compatible with Emerson and Thoreau of the Transcendentalists, I felt the spiritual center as an indwelling. The Christian idea of original sin was abandoned for the original blessedness of Genesis... "created in God's image." This fit with the Buddhist vision that we are born with all we need, we just have to come to realize and manifest it in our lives. The poems shared that sense of wonder and Oneness in the presence of the moment.

Neither Coming Nor Going

The light above the trees
falls through to yellowed leaves
spread on roofs near the lake
where mallards fly south.

    This time the music
    does not rush me.

    This time I hear
    each note, feel

harmonies climb,
dance inside the sound.

An egret stands and stares beyond my face
as my van and I glide down the road.
All is moving, all is here,
in this leaving/staying mind.

What I hope emerges in this book of poems is how central Nature is to this silent knowing and how an outlook can embrace seemingly contradictory tendencies. Paradox and mystery open the world. As Lorri would say, "Neither one, nor two, but both." Great doubt was replaced with acceptance of non-dualism and not-knowing. Ann's comment after a month of my being back home was, "I have to tell you. Since the retreat, you've become so much more open and calm. I like it." I felt it, too, and found this same spirit in the poems of fellow poet Stephen Conkle which were combined with my own in this dual book.

Ohio Zen: Poems (1990)

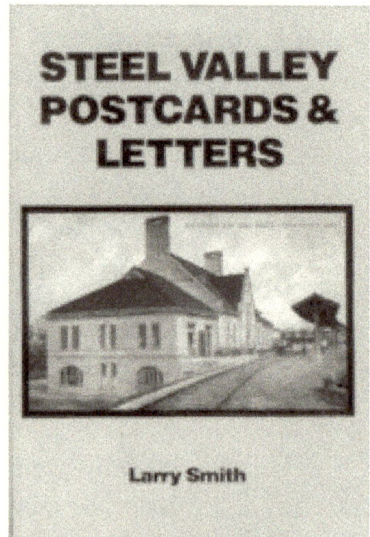

Steel Valley: Postcards & Letters (1992)

Life and art again became one in my next book *Steel Valley: Postcards and Letters*, a book of letter poems. The letters are not my own but fictional based on the voices of my Ohio Valley people and published appropriately by Youngstown's Pig Iron Press in 1992. It follows a long tradition of working-class writing in which the poet takes on the personality, life, and voice of another, a persona poem. Again, following John Keats advice, I witnessed how empathy opens creativity. More immediately, these poems were germinated from my buying old postcards for their historical reference and as visual stills for our film making on Ohio poets. However, in reading the short messages of lives scrolled on their backs, I saw how much could be suggested in so few words, the essence of poetry. Often when I would read from this book to audiences, someone would ask where had I found these letters, and I would try to explain that they were fiction but based upon the voices of my youth and my Ohio Valley sense of history and place. The titles would have the name, place, and date that they were to have been written, and so the form allowing me to honor the people of my time and place. A few came from a box of love letters from my mother to my father before they married young, a time when her mother was looking down on my father. After I showed them to my mother to read, she blushed yet granted me permission to adapt them in my book. One is entitled "Letter from Jean—Mingo Junction, 1941":

> Oh, Del, I know we're young
> like the sun rising
> and I know you have plans
> that I may be no part in.
> I know this and yet
> I can't help loving you.
>
> Forget what my mother said, please.

It's not what's in my heart.
It's what's in her head where
no one is ever good enough.

I watched you today in church
turn your head away.
You made your back hard
and blank as a headstone.
Yet, I know your soft eyes
and strong hands. I will never
think badly of you. Sometime soon
you may know how much
I've loved you. I pray for it.

A somewhat fictional projection of my sweet
Hungarian father-in-law John came in this poem of his
leaving school when young to help the family:

Letter from John—Follansbee, 1916

Today I walk in to town
got a job making glass
dollar a day.
Dollar a day make
five dollars a week,
pretty good for young boy
come from Hungary
two year ago.
I think
to help Mama some,
only thing is
I got to quit school.
I tell you
I miss them nuns
and the stories

in them books.
Like another world inside me now.
Someday I go back,
what you think?
I think someday
maybe.

Here I could project the lives of both of my parents caught in the tangle of their loving each other, and I could capture the quiet character of my working-class father-in-law. The cast of letter writers covers several decades and many working-class families, fulfilling a goal of creating a writing form to witness and reveal the value of each life. "In the simple grace of people/ we all learn to survive."

Chapter Twelve: First Fictions

Steel Valley helped me share my working-class life while it also took me deeper into the world of creative empathy in writing, and so my next two books were empathic writings of fiction *Beyond Rust: Novella and Stories* (Bottom Dog Press, 1995) and the novella sequel *Working It Out* (Ridgeway Press, 1998). *Beyond Rust* was my first attempt to project the Ohio Valley beyond family into the world of strikes and shut downs, violence and deaths. A steel worker's enemy is rust, and so the novella projects a community that is made stronger by dealing together with the mistreatment and loss of that industry. An underlying principle of my fiction is that of Sherwood Anderson, who declared that each person is a story worth telling, in fact many stories. In *Beyond Rust* all of the stories and narratives could be set in hometown Mingo Junction, though I often use the nearby steel town setting of Lorain, Ohio. Most are autobiographically based.

Bingo at the Mingo Show

There was a time when I just about *lived* at the Mingo Show, soaking up the soft matinee light as the screen glowed with the real dreams of cowboys and show girls, gangsters and gun molls, comics and heroes, or the semi-sweet tales of Disney animals or loving families that touched and informed my life. . . .

Fourteen cents was the ticket price for years at the Mingo Show, till they finally upped it to a dime and a nickel. So, we took back pop bottles, ran errands for neighbors, and went to the movies often. On Friday and Saturday *High Noon* might be showing, and on Sunday, Monday, and Tuesday *The Quiet Man* would play. In the middle of the week, on Wednesday and Thursday, you could catch a showing of *A Streetcar Named Desire*. The lives on the screen seemed to extend our own as stretched into the fresh anguish of Marlon Brando or James Dean. We packed it in together at the OK Corral with Burt Lancaster and Kirk Douglas. For working-class kids, we traveled a lot in our own hometowns.

Sometimes, if I had done my homework and if Grandma was going so that Mom had no sitter, I could go along for the midweek showing of a film like *Born Yesterday*. It would be dish and bingo night, and the lights would be on as the usher (some friend's older brother, or a kid who had graduated from his paper route) would hand us our gravy boats which Mom and Grandma would cradle on their laps beside me.

On bingo night after the first showing, the lights would come on. We could all suddenly see each other. The place would be packed with smiling neighbors and kids rubbing the sleep from their eyes. Then "Mingo Mike" Kendrach, the manager, would come out onto the stage with a couple of grinning ushers rolling in the bingo board and balls. He would tap the microphone a couple times and ask, "Is this on?" To which we would all shout back, "No, it's on!" and roar with laughter. Then he would smile and declare, "Good evening, everyone. And welcome to the Mingo Show." It seems now that the general response to this was a kind of relieved laughter. Then Mike would get serious as he announced, "Tonight, ladies and gentlemen, there will be fifty numbers called in our game. And I remind you that tonight's grand prize is ..." (There was silence here, just to be certain we knew the stakes.) " ...200 dollars!" Real sighs went up at the sound of the amount, for most of us had already spent it in our heads buying new refrigerators and bikes. Of course, this was before our state lotteries made winning outrageous amounts seem almost common. "Yes, 200 dollars is tonight's prize,"

Mingo Mike would declare, and I could watch my mom holding her card as she smiled down on me, as if to say, "Boy, wouldn't your father be surprised."

*   *   *

In the novella I create the young struggling couple of Maria and Marco. He is working his way to becoming a writer and witness of that life. It concludes with Marco's statement which is so much my own:

> Maybe what Dr. Franco says is right, someday this story will be published and lots of people read it. I'd like to do that for everyone. But it's already helped me. When I look around now, I see the life that's there in Ted and Marge or Mom and Dad, in their keeping family alive. It's in Esther and Jose and their fire for fairness and in me and sweet Maria working things out together. I see it in a young laughing Kenny or even in Janis struggling towards herself, in Rudy...It's in Angelina writing her young girl's life in Loran, Ohio, and in the old man in the blue coat gathering litter from around his building. In all of it is the sweet dignity of going on, of moving out from under the rock, even pushing it along. I know, because when I can write of it, it is enough.

In this story of the humble yet heroic figures of Marco and Maria I had created a base and a voice to write from, and so I used them again in my second novella, *Working it Out* (Ridgeway Press). Here Marco graduates from a community college and becomes a teacher and a writer, and Maria is pregnant with their first child. The setting of Lorain, Ohio, a close approximation to Mingo Junction, focuses on a declining steel mill town. As author Jim Daniels so kindly put it, "*Working It Out* is a rich, moving story of one man's attempts to work out what we all have to work out, regardless of our personal histories—the precious balance between where we've come from and where we're going, between the demands of work and family, between who we are and who we want to be." That very much describes the book's focus and my own essential struggle, yet it is Annabel Thomas who captures the book's hopeful vision. "Yet the fierce, enduring love between Marco and Maria, the supportive caring and loyalty of their families as the birth of their first child draws near, give us, against all odds, blessed hope for the future of humanity." The book rose out of my sense of life in a working-class town, the trust of family, and in the work and hope of education. Of note, my own daughter Laura was pregnant at the time with our first grandchild, Rosa. We had flown out to Seattle for her outdoor wedding with Allen Frost, and so their lives too are projected into these characters and local settings.

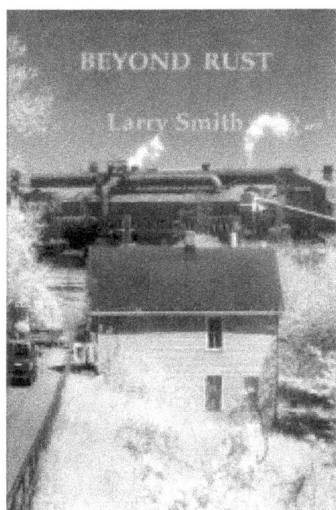

Beyond Rust (1995)   *Working It Out* (1998)

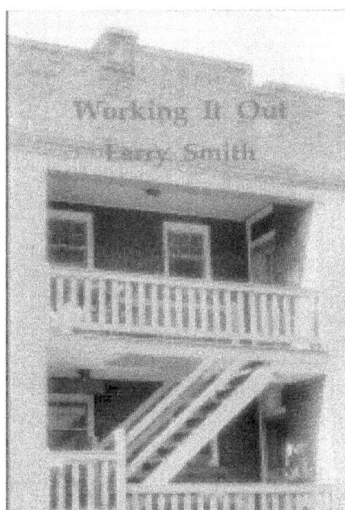

I felt that I was able in these books to work my past and future into a present setting. It was satisfying to see the book reach a deserving audience and being used in college classes, notably in Detroit and Cleveland.

Larry in Huron at railroad tracks (1998)

Chapter Thirteen: Life in Translation & Channeling

That same year, 1998, I had been working with a woman from Taiwan on a book of Zen poem translations from the Chinese. In 1996 Mei Hui Huang had moved from Taiwan to nearby Catawba, where her husband C.T. imported and sold yachts, and her two children attended high school in Ohio. She became my college student in order to improve her English language skills. Surprisingly like me, she was a mix of Buddhism and Protestantism and skilled in the Zen arts of poetry, but also in painting and flower arranging. These skills she shared in an "Introduction to Humanities" course which I was then teaching. As friends we began doing translations of the ancient Chinese poets, and though she urged me to learn the Chinese language, I failed at that and so relied on her for first versions into English which I then moved into American English poems subject to her approval. When she and her husband moved to California and eventually back to Taiwan, we continued this work via e-mail.

Our first bi-lingual book *Chinese Zen Poems: What Hold Has this Mountain?* (Bottom Dog Press 1998) sold well in America and in Taiwan. Translation requires more than finding language equivalents; most of the Chinese poets of the Tang period write in an intimate personal voice, and so the translator must "become" the poet in understanding and outlook. The simplicity, depth, and openness of these ancient poems drew me further into a Zen outlook on writing and life as a means of being in the "here now" moment. Though Zen can seem mysterious to an outsider, all of its practices (contemplative and meditative sitting, walking, poetry) lead to the single goal of being more fully alive. In my eyes Buddha was not a mystical divine being, but a real person who had awakened (a "Buddha") and sought to share that awareness through the meditation practice.

A decade later Mei Hui and I would work to complete a second book of Zen translations. Rather than including a wide diversity of poets such as Tu Fu, Po Chu Hui, Wang Wei, and others as we did in *Chinese Zen Poems*, in this new book we focused on the Chinese written poems of one Japanese poet, Taigu Ryôkan (1758–1831). For years we had casually worked on translating his poems with only a vague sense of doing it as a book. My love for Ryôkan's bare bones verse had drawn me into an intimate sense of his life. His journal poems spoke to us both in this resonant way. Sometimes referred to as a hermit monk, Ryôkan was in fact most sociable, welcoming guests to his humble mountain hut, regularly playing with the town's children, wearing out his begging bowl and walking staff. Nicknamed "the Great Fool," he could be both humble with others and demanding when it came to Zen practice. His humility is apparent in this journal poem:

> I have spent many free and idle days in ignorance.
> Beside me I keep a single cane. My clothes
> have melted away like threads of smoke.
> Facing a blank window, I hear the midnight rain.
> In the heart of spring, I bounce a ball in the street.
> If anyone should ask who I am
> I show myself a great fool in a foolish age.

This life of simplicity is a clear choice for Ryôkan, much like the intention which near contemporary Henry David Thoreau declared while living at Walden Pond, "I wanted to live deep and suck out all the marrow of life, to live so sturdily and Spartan-like as to put to rout all that was not life, to cut a broad swath and shave close, to drive life into a corner, and reduce it to its lowest terms." Ryôkan also writes to correct the corruption of those living a false Buddhist practice. In "My Hut" he concludes:

> The sun comes out, and I mend my robes.
> The moon comes out, and I read Buddhist poems.
>
> I have nothing to report, my friends.
> If you would find the way,
> Stop chasing after so many things.

That last line, "Stop chasing after so many things," spoke profoundly to me. So easily we become distracted, watching what others do and think, and so take on pretense. The act of translating these works was part of my contemplative practice. And so, in 2008 Mei Hui Huang and I put together a tri-lingual translation in Chinese, Japanese, and English, *The Kanshi Poems of Taigu Ryôkan* (Bottom Dog Press 2008). It was a book that met with my life. Ryôkan remains a model and a spirited ally, and our book became a staple for those who admire his work.

Chinese Zen Poems (1998)

The Kanshi Poems of Taigu Ryokan (2008)

Among contemporary American writers who most expressed these basic values is the poet Gary Snyder. I embraced this organic vision of life where nature and place are a part of you and you of it, like a plant rooted in the earth yet ripening to fulfillment. This vision of finding the true self flowed into the poems I was writing then and now.

Channeling Thoreau

As I often write from within the sensed voice of another, I next chose to become Henry David Thoreau and write the personal poems which he never wrote. I would do so in a fictional journal, *Thoreau's Lost Journal: Poems* (Westron Press 2001). Drawn to Thoreau's personal story—the loss of his brother, his admiration then rivalry with the older philosopher-poet Emerson, his infatuation with Emerson's wife Lidian, and his sense of loneliness as well as solitude—I sought to project the person of Henry Thoreau from within myself. When a friend declared that I was "channeling" Thoreau in this book, I accepted that, though to me it was much like translating him as person, a kind of method acting whereby you must get inside the character of another to speak.

Afternoon in which Henry David
Measures out the Moments

Last night I dreamed my father
sitting on the old porch at noon
cutting pencils in the light.
His sure hands were quick on the wood
and yet his eyes were closed.
And I turned and walked away
into the shade inside the trees.

I carried this dream to breakfast
where Mother served questions

with my tea: "Where, Henry,"
she asked across the table oak
as my bread crumbs lay in rows,
"will we get the rent this month?
Can you please, son, think ahead?"
I read the lines around her eyes,
yet turned again to face the woods.

Now, in deep green I smell
the cool of running rapids
and drink the shadow light of day.
Each vision calls me, robs the air—
a past I know, a future I would not.
I bend and pick the ground apples,
its simple weight the moment's measure;
with open eyes I bite and know
sweet taste of what is now.

Thoreau's Lost Journal

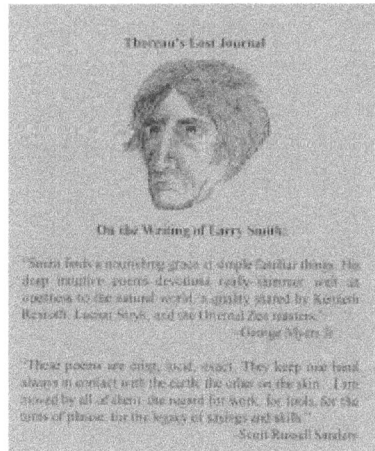

Cover art by Zita Sodeika

Note how artist Zita Sodeika appropriately blended my image with Thoreau's here. We had become one for this book.

Chapter Fifteen: Memoirs and Mature Poems

In January of 2003 my official retirement from college teaching arrived, though I continued to teach a literature course each semester till 2010. Retirement gave me time to work on the big anthologies of Bottom Dog Press: *Family Matters* (2005) on literature treating family done with Ann as co-editor, another *Come Together: Imagine Peace* (2008) on nonviolence and peace with Ann and poet Phil Metres as my co-editors. An earlier one, *America Zen* (2004), included new Zen poets co-edited with poet and friend Ray McNiece. In each we sought a close sense of what would resonate with a wider audience. If either Ann or I really didn't like a poem or feel that it didn't connect with readers, it was not used. Ann, whose background included family therapy, was sharp on personal relevance. We worked well together, and though both Phil and Ray brought in other fine writers, as expected, we struggled with both the selection and arrangement of the poems. All of these books went into second and third printings and kept the press solvent.

I had continued to write my way through this early period of retirement, and so in 2005 Ridgeway Press of Michigan published my first book of memoir writing, *Milldust and Roses: Memoirs*. With a photograph of hometown Mingo Junction on the front cover and personal family photos within, the book ran chronologically through my life, using poems, prose-poems, and personal essays to reveal my life vision while capturing its development. Expressive in approach, the book followed the memoir form of selective memories and so lacked much of the literal facts of my life. In the book's introduction, I acknowledged my natural subjective memory. When I queried my sister Janis as to her response to the book, she wrote me that "Yes, I like the book very much, but honestly I remember more roses and less mill dust." While I understood her short and pointed review, for me the book's images and their meanings were forever bound to experiences that were most a part of me. Because my previous books of personal poems were typically autobiographical, in composing this book I garnered much from these previous writings, revamping some poems into prose. "The Silence of Tools" suggests the basic approach and mixed tones of the book:

The Silence of Tools

My father worked in basement silence, bent like a crave over his work bench, tools in hand, thinking his way through with them, connecting cause and effect till there was no room left for fault or waste. Near him stood the old coal furnace he kept, the coal on the floor, three footsteps away.

And I sat on the steps beneath the hanging light watching his hands, straining for him to be set free, to come back upstairs with mother and me, sit on the back porch together as the mill roared softly by the river.

But no, he seemed to love it there below in the silence he harvested from tools. And I would go up to my room and swim alone through lost rivers of words.

The most personally accessible book I had done, it gained some strong reviews and was shared through public readings and book signings. In these events I truly felt exposed, yet I accepted this as part of any writer's role—to share wholly the truth of a life. One colleague at school stopped to ask me how I was doing with my prostate cancer, and though I felt somewhat vulnerable at her knowing this, I also felt satisfied at sharing the unspoken. As I write in the author's preface: "One of my spiritual fathers, Henry David Thoreau, asks of every writer 'a simple and sincere account of his life.' I attempt to give that here. If our message lies in our intention, my hope in telling my life is to confirm the lives of other."

Milldust and Roses includes my dealing with prostate cancer in the section entitled "Season of Cancer" which seeks to serve the universal through the intimate and personal. As many of us come to know, a serious medical condition can throw you back on your whole life, as this cancer clearly did. The positive is that you can come to appreciate everything and everyone in new and deeper ways. "The Season of Cancer" section of *Milldust and Roses* registers many of those life awakenings, as in this poem.

The Spiral Walk

I take the path into the woods knowing that darkness is falling, and all about me the songs are rising—Nature eternal and my own—echoing.

Out in the pond stands a great blue heron— steely gray in the silver light of dusk where the moon coming up meets the sun going down.

And it is not the bird of Nature books nor the one of mythic poems. The blue heron standing in moonlit water is the blue heron in moonlit water. And the one watching from shore is the one watching from shore.

I cannot hold this moment any longer than itself, and it passes through me: *water in my hands/ air around me.* I must let go and return to my town, my house, its lights, my life where phones ring and the dog needs let out.

> I taste this hunger and sorrow, this joy
> and trust, knowing the risk of loss and the truth
> that only comes by touching all that I am, the
> heart open to itself.

This learned acceptance brought me through a storm much wiser and more whole. For me and my family dealing with cancer proved a long and mellow wisening in both the head and heart. I wrote some fifty poems dealing with cancer which rose from my journaling of thoughts and feelings. This method of treating it through honest writing brought it up close—for me and hopefully for others who had or would face cancer or any disabling disease.

The memoir also allowed me to tell some of the family stories as in this account.

Running into the Night

The stadium lights recorded our triumph. The mile relay was always run last and almost always determined the outcome of the meet. Outside the fence, the deep roar of the blast furnaces and the quick clash of the freight trains marked the events. I and my brother would run legs three and four that night.

I remember sliding off my sweats, folding them onto the bench, then jumping up and down to keep warm in the April air. "Stay up with him," coached my brother, "And if you can get a lead, kick it home." On the side of the track we practiced handing off the baton with Jim and Tom. We drew our lane, then paced around to keep loose. Weeks ago I had pulled a muscle on the final curve and had to limp my way across the finish line, winning the meet, then be carried into the locker-room.

Neither of us said anything, but we kept checking the crowd for Dad's red jacket. Our eyes told each other he must have pulled a double or the car had broken down. The coach called us over, "Okay, we're behind again by one point. It's all up to you guys." We read the ground, each other's eyes. "Just run a good race," he called and walked away.

That night we were invincible. Don't ask me why. Each runner stepped out ahead at least a stride, so that I stretched it out to a good yard. Dave took the stick in his hand coming up and kicked it all the way, under four minutes. My lungs were still burning as he passed the flag pole releasing the roar of the crowd. We had brought it home like we never would again..

When Uncle Ray came into the locker room, we were still in the showers singing "La Bamba." He came over to David who then turned to me. "Dad's in the hospital. His appendix burst." We were dressed and out of there in five minutes. Uncle Ray drove like a maniac up the Steubenville streets to the Ohio Valley Hospital. "Go on in," he called through the dark. "I'll park this thing."

I think it was then I started hating hospitals— their fatal numbness, the sickening antiseptic smell, the hallways all full of dread.

When we first saw Dad I thought he was dead. He lay there so pale and weak with needles and tubes running into his arms like a sick carburetor. Mute and cold, I wanted someone's words. *Orphans,* I thought to myself, though it didn't make sense, and then Mom was hugging us. "He's recovering. He was hit hard with it while rushing home to get to your damn track meet." I took a breath, the first it seemed in hours. "My God,"

she said, "Look at you. You're white as a ghost!"
Everyone stared at my naked face so that I could not
hide my pain or my sorrow. When she asked about the
track meet, I still couldn't talk. David and I just stood
there mute by Dad's bedside until he opened his eyes.

By rendering this family story of triumph and tragedy, of
joy and pain, I felt able to suggest the ambivalence of life
that had become so familiar to me. Ambivalence and family
and community strength are the overriding themes of that
book. *Milldust and Roses* went through two printings, with
Ridgeway Press and then Bottom Dog Press.

Milldust and Roses: Memoirs
(2005)

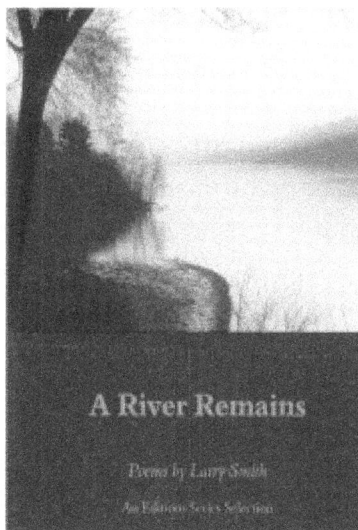

A River Remains: Poems
(2006)

**Larry from cover photo taken on
40ᵗʰ anniversary by Ann (2006)**

Six years later in 2006, I collected my poems into the large book *A River Remains: Poems* for WordTech Press of Cincinnati. The book's subdivisions which I struggled to discover are essential layers of my life and writing, stones in my river of stones. "After" goes into the years right 'after' retirement; "Cut and Stacked, Tanka and Haiku" present the Zen vision of Nature that I had come to embrace; "Native Grounds" covers youthful times in the Ohio Valley; "Standing in Muddy Waters" speaks of the suffering and eventual losses we all face; "The Cancer Poems, Living with It" carries the story of facing cancer into the present as a cancer survivor; "Traveling, Taking Leave at Daybreak" connects Nature and place with our being more alive; and finally "Our Intentions, Waking to It" presents the many converging spirit pathways of my life.

WordTech, the publisher of *A River Remains*, was directed by Kevin Walzer and his wife Lori as another Ohio publisher who had for some time celebrated fine Midwest authors. Both their press and Bottom Dog Press could not have happened without the guidance of friend Bob Fox, who had launched and run Carpenter Press in the 1970s and who directed the literature division of the Ohio Arts Council. Born a week apart, Bob and I became best friends until he passed away from cancer in March of 2005. We had reached that age in our 60s where we found our mentors in our peers. In one poem I write of walking out with Bob into the woods near a pond and finding a bunch of "old guys" spotting eagles. Only later at home, as I told Ann of the incident, did I realize that these "old guys" were our own age. We were all old guys. Bob and our friendship helped me deal with that, and he became the subject of several writings in the "Standing in Muddy Waters" section of *A River Remains*. This poem indicates our closeness and our vulnerability:

This Day

> While visiting a Columbus library
> I learn of my friend's cancer
> from his wife standing strong,
> though her voice trembles when she talks.
> I take her hand, look into her eyes,
> and do not ask how long.
>
> On the drive home, I think of him:
> born a week apart, brothers under the skin,
> his fingers dancing over guitar strings,
> his voice telling us an old story.
> I touch the warm pain of knowing,
> then disappear into the road.

As the poem suggests, our closeness was that of being kindred brothers, watching our children grow, loving our wives, caring about writing and helping it spread, while also facing our inevitable aging and death. I had lived through my cancer, but sadly Bob would not. Our caring is indicated in this poem:

Writing in the Middle of the Night
For Bob

A friend a long way off
is passing through the
final stages of cancer,
a path he'd walked
years ago with his wife.
It comes and takes you,
turns your cells to purple gel.
He knows all that
as he lies tonight
cocooned from the consuming pain.

I am so speechless now
I can only send him peace—
all the cannabis plants of
Athens County during the 60s
when he wrote those wonder stories
of old farmers and tool salesmen
in those backwoods—
all the music his fingers danced
out of guitar and piano strings—
all the plants he grew
out of rocky Appalachian hills—
all the writing of others
he farmed in Ohio, his second home—

I pray he feels the love of families
gone ahead and left behind.
I stand in his broad circle of friends
hear his breath upon the land
and wait.

Old friend I love you
like a brother.

And then...the word comes:
He is gone.

I can't talk or write...

Kate calls to say he's been cremated...
He is ashes now,
and I cannot swallow that down.
For how can he be gone
so quick and final
when he is so with me still?

Old friend, may I never forget
your smile, your voice.

At Bob's memorial service, as he had wished, they handed out his CD of guitar, piano, and vocals, Bob doing his blues songs for all of us others. I play it when I need to be close to him and myself.

Bob Fox

Chapter Fifteen: Author Film Appreciations

Another good friend died in May of 2007, Tom Koba, co-director and co-producer of our two documentary films done on Ohio authors James Wright and Kenneth Patchen. Tom and I had been friends for twenty years. For those film projects I managed the grants from the Ohio Arts Council and the Ohio Humanities Council, and wrote the scripts which, like life itself, became adapted by the reality of actual filming. Tom was way ahead of me in the art of film making, I simply loved the power of film to treat reality. I remember starting to shoot *James Wright's Ohio* by filming my young daughter Suzanne walking down the sidewalk outside of my parents' house. I turned to Tom and asked, "Any direction?" He stared back, "You're the director," and I, "No, you're the director." And so we laughed in the street, called "cut" then worked it out as co-directors, though Tom was clearly the real filmmaker. Upfront he told me, "Listen, you can carry the camera and help set up shots, but I'll do all the shooting," and so he did. I was also the one to get permission to film people and places, a task that met with challenges and rewards.

Both films were shot in main or part in none other than Mingo Junction. Here the steel mills remained active and so the town provided apt living sets right before us; the actors were pretty much people playing themselves and so conveying the life there. Young James was a neighborhood kid, Wright's father was Uncle Ron Mitchell who had worked the mills most of his life, my mother was Wright's mother, etc. My mother-in-law gave us lodging and fed us well. Not too surprising, the locals offered us advice on where to shoot, some going so far as to suggest methods of shooting and editing; they had had the big *The Deerhunter* filmed in Mingo. One humorous event came when we showed up to film a Mingo High School football game, and because we were driving the university van, we were given full permission to film, assuming that we were college scouts. The volunteered efforts of many and their cheap labor, helped us complete the film.

For me there was a deep satisfaction in knowing that I had found a way to capture and present this working-class life. Eight months later we premiered our film in a Mingo school assembly hall, at Firelands College, at the James Wright Poetry Festival in Martins Ferry, Ohio, and then it was shown on Public Broadcasting channels and distributed by Bottom Dog Press. The same pattern was followed with our next film, "Kenneth Patchen: An Art of Engagement," filmed and premiered around Warren and Youngstown, Ohio, though also shot in San Francisco and Palo Alto.

I had come to know Tom as an area filmmaker in the early 1980s when we worked together to create an experimental film festival at the college. We had an immediate bond as working-class artists. Tom had made his first feature film while a high school student in Lorain, Ohio. He graduated from Ohio University with a degree in art and film, taught art in high school, and eventually became the director of audio-visual services at Firelands College. Then he left school work to film and produce training films and historical documentaries of our area. We often met at his country studio where he constructed film sets. Sitting among his gadgets and stacks of video cartridges, we would laugh together and plot a quiet radicalism in our area. Tragically and ironically on the day we were to hold a rally for universal health care coverage, Tom, who had avoided seeking health treatment because he lacked insurance, died of a heart attack, an irony that would not have been lost on him. Though we had other film projects planned, his death ended my career in film making.

Filmmakers Tom Koba and Larry Smith inside Wheeling Steel Mill, Mingo Junction (1989), photo by Paul Ferguson

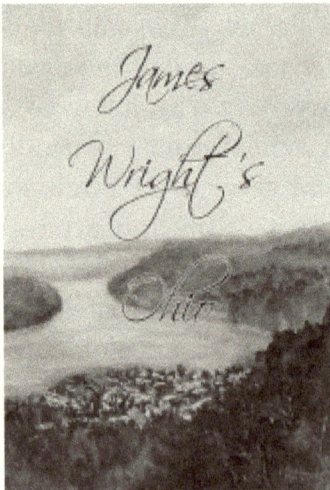

James Wright's Ohio **film**

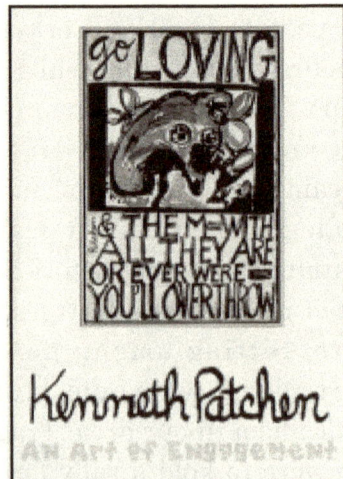

Kenneth Patchen: An Art of Engagement **film**

Chapter Sixteen: Later Fictions—Voices and Sagas

The deaths of friends and family can bring sadness but also reflection and insight in looking back over our actions and obsessions. I could recognize my way of listening to the voices of others and, through empathy, write of them. An overheard conversation in a restaurant or elevator could lead to a whole story in my head. It seems no surprise that my next work was a collection of short stories written as monologues, each in the voice of a singular character. *Faces and Voices* (2006), like the poems of *Steel Valley: Postcards and Letters*, goes inside of characters and has them talk their story and thereby reveal their life in story form and in the act of their telling. My ear for voices began from being a child and standing in line at the Mingo Show, listening to the old Italian or Hungarian women gossip, the young black mother care over her sons, the pretty Polish girl who sold popcorn flirting. Everyone holds their story, sometimes many of them, and a writer's mission is to capture and release that story. And so I wrote, trusting that these stories of young and old would come to life for others as they did for me. Perhaps writing dialogue for the two films encouraged this, but also there was the ease of writing fiction over the strain of seeking and managing financing in the making of a film. Though clearly the films shown in local premiers and over the Public Broadcasting System had a larger impact, in these written stories it was a matter of me being you being us.

Here is a comic sample entitled "Confessions of a Class Poet" in which the main character shares his addiction as in an AA type meeting for poets:

Hello. My name is Edgar Allen. And uh...I'm a class poet.

I started writing the stuff back in junior high, scribbling into my notebook at nights alone in my room. I'd hide it in my underwear drawer back then. I'd lie to my parents, say I was doing math homework or writing a report, but I can admit it now—it was always poems, one after another—getting high on them alone in my room and hiding it in a drawer when I was through.

Then one night my freshman year in high school I was out with friends and we ended up at a coffeehouse ...they were doing an Open-Mic poetry reading and, at my friend's coaching, I got up and read my first poem out in public. I had been carrying it in my coat pocket for weeks. They egged me on, and the crowd ate it up. I was hooked—I was...a class poet—I can say it now— writing poems for friends, the school newspaper, and then the school's literary magazine *A Pocket Full of Dreams*.

Others heard about me and before long I was writing poems for them for their girlfriends, eventually writing the class poem, the class song. I was in above my head and I couldn't stop myself—I was addicted.

By using fiction's methods of exaggeration and inflation I was able to create a voice to portray the obsessions of myself and others. As I learned from my mother, being able to laugh at one's self-absorptions is one way to be released from them. *Faces and Voices* follows a loose life chronology moving from youth to age, but the characters are each unique and not related except by place. We have a teenage store clerk, an auto repairman, a young Buddhist, a support group director, an Italian mother, a frustrated roofer, an old pacifist, and many more, each with a story to tell.

In "The Old Pacifist" I projected a character based on my meeting with activist David Dellinger and my knowing local pacifist Bill Wright. Dellinger had gone to prison for his pacifist views; Bill had been beaten as a union organizer. The character is being interviewed by a young writer for *The Progressive* magazine. On his going to jail he says,

> What's the price of anything really? Thoreau says the cost is how much life you'll sacrifice for it. He was talking human economics see, trying to get you to value your life before you spend it, but I take it another way. Your sacrifice gives it value. It's moral economics. What did my going to jail in New York and later Chicago amount to? It's hard to measure, but I like to think those days and nights alone in that dark cell made a kind of human difference in the larger way of things. Do you get me? Do you see what I'm saying? I'm not going to be around much longer singing this song, see. That's why I'm talking to you here; that's why I wrote that book.

Though I continued to write a couple poems a week, and to translate the poems of Ryokan with Mei Hui Huang, my focus had shifted to the narrative of my family and life. I had always dreamed of writing the Smith family saga. Original research begun 30 years ago by my brother David and enhanced by my son Brian's internet research tools had reconstructed the details of our Smith and Putnam family genealogies. What struck us all as we scanned the dates and names of these relatives never met was the absence of any story. And so as a writer and someone who needed story, I launched into a retelling and creating of those stories through autobiographic fiction. The first book, *The Long River Home: A Novel* (2009), went back as far as we could trace to the Smith family following Civil War times when we knew great-grandfather Andrew Smith had been born. Try as we would, we could not locate any birth or ancestry records for this most colorful figure of our clan. When Brian, Suzanne, and I visited the Smith property in McArthur, Ohio, and talked with the grandsons, we only heard stories of Andrew's wildness and Ernie's strictness. Fiction completes where facts leave off and the imagination seeks to fill in. For example, his lack of records suggested to me that he was an orphan, which fit with the time and place in this country as there were many war orphans after the Civil War. Where would he have been taken—but to Xenia, Ohio to the Ohio Soldiers' and Sailors' Orphans Home begun in 1869. How would he have come to work on a German farmer's property in McArthur, Ohio, but through adoption as a teenage "farm hand," as he was in fact listed in the 1870 census by Henry Eustler. In a few years he would marry daughter Mary Jane Eustler and be given a single acre of their 100 acre farm at the back, back corner. Why the worst acre on that farm? There another story began. In this way I was able to use the facts to project a great-grandfather and a great-grandmother I never knew. I could now do this as well for Andrew's son Ernie, my grandfather, who died when I was two.

In a dedicated way I was filling in my own sense of family and heritage. The writing was satisfying and the story evolved as family members moved from southern to eastern Ohio for work in industry along the Ohio River. Census documents declared that Andrew spent his last years as a "barber" while living in son Ernie's house in Mingo. When my mother and father appeared with their story of youthful romance, it felt so good to be close with them again. The closer the novel came to my father and mother's lives, the more autobiographical it became, yet always I felt the freedom of fiction to "fill in" the story in order to make it felt by others. By the time it was done, I sensed that the book cried for a genealogy of characters, and so I created one for the fictional McCall family on Ancestry.com. I even received a message from a real McCall member saying he thought we were related. The fictional genealogy which appears at the back of that novel parallels much of the real Smith heritage.

The book took two years to write, then it circulated to publishers for about a year till I resolved to make it a Bottom Dog Press book. It fit so perfectly with the values of the press: working-class, Appalachian, with a strong sense of person and place. After a couple fellow writers read and edited it, it appeared in hard and soft cover in 2009. I sent copies to all of my children and to my brother and sisters with a note reminding them that it was fiction and my projected story; they were welcome to write their own. When daughter Laura living out in Washington state read it, she called back to say that she loved it, but asked, "Dad, how much is fiction and how much is real?" I thought about that only for a moment and answered back, "Well, honey, it's all real, and I can no longer separate it that way." I explained that I wasn't being smart with her, but that truth was larger than fact. I also offered to send her the Smith-Putnam genealogy if she wanted those facts, yet I warned, "But the story isn't there. It has to live inside of you as it does me."

Though I thought I had finished with the Smith saga, a year later I found myself writing the sequel, taking the young boy from the first novel to college in the turbulent late 1960s. The setting was in the heart of Appalachia—first in a steel mill town, of course, and then at Ohio University and a nearby commune which the young man helps found around 1968. Though clearly a projection of myself into this world, in fact I had not lived there or in a commune, but for cultural background I had lived through these times with Ann while a graduate student at Kent State University. Later I had come to know Athens through my daughter Suzanne's schooling there, and through good friends Denny and June who had each been part of a commune around the late 1960s. I explored extensive readings and films on communal living, among the best a memoir, *Sleeping where I Lie*, by actor Peter Coyote who had lived in several communes. He told of the successes and failures of communal life. For my own book's thematic core I sought to establish the validity of questioning, of accepting the not knowing of experience, and of seeking and living out alternative lifestyles. I did not seek to idealize the commune, but to show the basic values behind such alternative communities.

The novel is also a love story of the two main characters who come from a working-class town to join with new allies to create "The Free Farm" commune in the Appalachian foothills. The couple deal with the pull of family and hometown, while also confronting issues of drugs, free love, freeloaders, the war in Vietnam, and with basic survival in those southern Ohio hills. To their aid come the local farming families, who override their own fears and distrust of outsiders with basic compassion and down home knowhow and sharing. A year after publication at a conference on Appalachia, I met several folks who lived in Southern Ohio communes then and who felt that I had captured well their struggles and spirit.

The Long River Home (2009)   **The Free Farm (2011)**

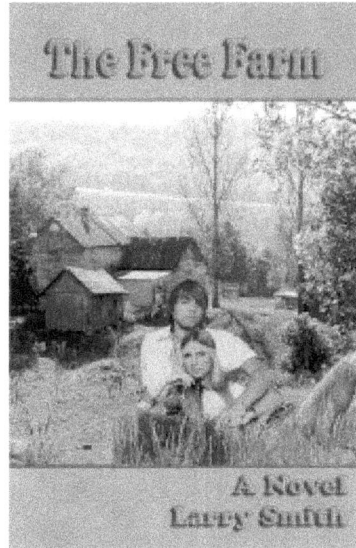

At this same time period (2010-2011) I was deep into a research and writing project that would bring me close to home again. For over a decade I had been urged by my parents' good friend Darlene Hoff to write the book of Mingo Junction. She and Jane Novotny had done the first history in the late 1960s, combining vintage photos with historical narratives. But the town was 40 years older now, and so Darlene urged an update. Arcadia Publishing, which does several series of historical photo books, was open to a proposal if I included a local person to co-author it. My brother was no longer local, and so I immediately turned to Guy Mason, my old classmate, fellow basketball player, doo-wop singer, and retired dentist. Guy had kept his old office and used it as a rare book dealership and local archive. He was also the unofficial town historian, often decorating his storefront windows with historical photo-posters of the town. We had stayed in touch and after convincing him that we could work together on this, he anchoring the local research and I working at editing the text, we were a team. As it turned out we shared both of these tasks, the most enjoyable being the talk with local people who had kept photo albums or could tell town and school and business history from their perspective. Research at the area library in Steubenville provided almost nothing except some important writing on the schools. Darlene's book was the most helpful. At first Guy and I would meet in the morning and head out on original research to talk with business owners, church people, those at the senior center across the street from Guy's shop.

Arcadia Publishing has a formula for such photo history books, and so we followed a pattern of treating the churches, the schools, the businesses, local heroes, and, my favorite, the people of the town. In Mingo everyone keeps track of families and their members. You can't begin to talk unless you can connect the person with the listener. Ex. "You know the Carocci family, they lived over on Hunkey Hill by the water tower. The father worked down at Dugan's Pool Hall. The mother was a Ferroni, went to school with my brother Al...etc." And so it was extremely important to us and our readers that we get the images and names of people into the book and that we spell them right. After looking at many of the other books by Arcadia, we were convinced that we did not want to do a book about buildings but of people standing together and facing the reader. We also included colorful stories of locals telling the town's brief skirt with fame as the setting for most of the shooting of the film *The Deer Hunter*, winner of the Academy Award as Best Picture in 1978. Suddenly Robert DeNiro and Meryl Streep and director Michael Cimino were living and working in the town along with a crew. Many locals were hired as extras, including one bartender whose bar still holds the sign in the window, "I was the bartender in *The Deer Hunter*." That and many other stories grace the book *Mingo Junction* which opens with my lines: "It's a long time between trains now,/ but we know one will arrive.// In the simple grace of people/ we all learn to survive." As with most of my writing, I could not have written the book until I myself had aged into it and gained a larger perspective.

When we held the local book signing, sponsored by the Junior Woman's Club of Mingo Junction, the gymnasium of Hills School was packed. Guy and I talked of the book and thanked townspeople, then showed a slide-show of photos from the book. When we showed the image of the long defunct Mingo Show, the crowd burst out in a roar of applause that sent a tingle up my arms. We sold over 120 books that day, the most I had ever sold as a writer or publisher at one time. The book would be available at local markets, history and gift shops, and at Guy's storefront book place. We had touched the heart of the town and offered some healing. If we could not project a story beyond the mill's closing and its future dismantling, so be it. The book proudly held up the town's history and strength of character. "Through good times and bad, Mingo Junction survives as a hardworking town."

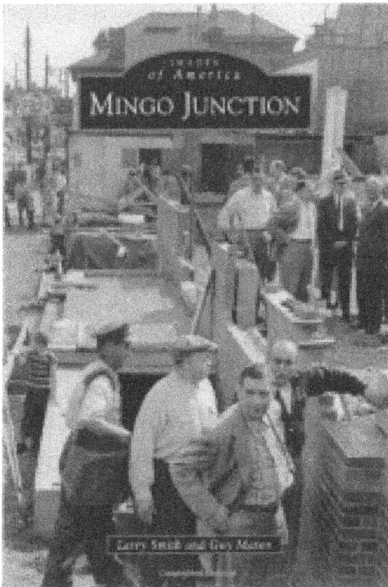

Book cover of *Mingo Junction* (2011) site of new city building in 1956

**The Deer Hunter Actors Meryl Streep, Rob DeNiro,
with Director Michael Cimino, Mingo 1978**

Chapbook Reflections

During these later years, I would write two poetry chapbooks. One projects Buddhism onto contemporary America, *Tu Fu Comes to America* (2010) using the voice of a Chinese Buddhist immigrant arriving in Cleveland, Ohio, and another captures the personal journey of my own spiritual life, *Each Moment All* (2012), both from March Street Press. When Rob Bixby, publisher of March Street Press, died along with the press in 2013, the books were picked up by Bottom Dog Press. *Each Moment All* is my blend of Buddhism and Christianity written after I had officially joined the Catholic Church in 2011 with Ann as my sponsor. For me there was no converting, only a convergence of faiths and an acceptance of mystery. I sense that the act of prayer is most often a silent meditation, and so meditation can also be prayer. Here are two sample poems:

Sitting with Him at the Meditation Center

We sit together on cushions,
the sun setting outside the windows
our room full of soft candlelight.

> *May I be filled with loving kindness.*
> *May I be well.*
> *May I be peaceful and at ease.*
> *May I be happy.*

This wish for ourselves and world
leans us into our days.
Our silence wraps around us
as we begin this night
bringing the faces of others
we have feared and loved before us,
sending Metta love to all.

> *May you be filled with loving kindness.*
> *May you be well.*
> *May you be peaceful and at ease.*
> *May you be happy.*

Gently guided I bring forth
the face of my father
gone now twenty-five years:
rugged brows in the rounded face
of a worker, his dark earnest eyes
neither asking nor answering—
my heart, my heart, my throat, my eyes,
soft tears within my breath.

> *With each breath the heart opens.*
> *With each breath the mind returns.*

I have passed him now with my years
and see his strong-soft face
as the friend he has become.

May you be filled with loving kindness.

Not only do I find myself praying the basic Metta Prayer of
compassion here, but I'm able to integrate it with the vision
of my father and early faith. Another mellow poem
frequently reprinted is this one in which I emerge through
gentle contemplation into a place of compassion and
acceptance.

Walking a Field into Evening

For learned books, I read the grasses.
For reputation, a bird calls my name.
I cross a stone bridge with the pace of dusk.
At the meadow gate, six cows meditate.

For decades I ran my mind up hill and down;
now idleness tells me what is near.
An arrow of wild geese crosses the sky,
my body still, my feet firm on the ground.

We age like trees now, watch our seedlings
take wind or grow around us.
I'm going to mark my books lightly
with a pencil. When someone wants
to take my picture, I'll walk towards them
and embrace.

No more arguments,
just heart sense, or talk about nothing.
Take long walks in the woods at dawn and dusk,

breathe in the damp musty air,
learn to listen before I die.

In this humbling vision I share the scale of life, finding acceptance of others, myself, and my paths. Its lament to learn to listen well remains one of my continuing challenges and goals.

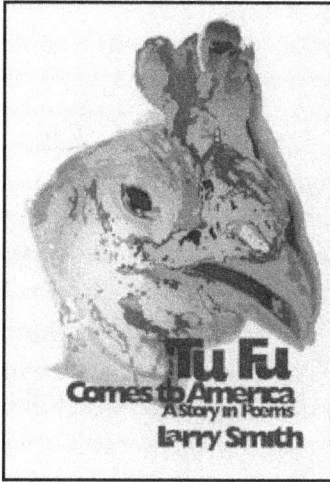

Tu Fu Comes to America:
A Story in Poems (2010)

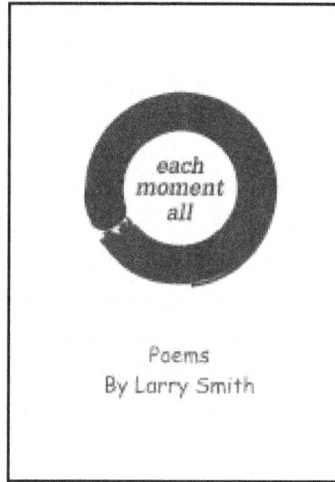

Each Moment All: Poems
(2011)

Chapter Seventeen: Salutations in Lake Winds

As life presents itself and I am open and aware, the poems keep coming. More and more they evolve through relationships with family, parents and grandparents, but especially with grandchildren, each a unique stone on the rip-rap of my life. Retirement simply meant having more time in the moment, though less in the long run. I could sit on the floor and let grandson Dylan show me how to play with trains again. I could make jokes with Maya to loosen and sharpen her grip on girlhood. I could let Adam teach me how to fish off the pier and keep track of book sales, and allow myself to learn cooking from his younger brother Alex. Cousins Alyssa and Zoe are each about the same age, and each little rebels and huggers. Though time being with Laura's Rosa and Rustle living in Bellingham is all too short, on visits and e-mail Ann and I could breathe in their character and connect by our quiet listening. We seek to be there for them in ways our grandparents were seldom able to do. They and their parents are the subject of many of the poems in my *Lake Winds: Poems* collection of 2014.

Other sections of that book include "Nature," "Bill's Poems" treating the aging of my old friend Bill Wright and myself, the love of a good woman in Ann, and the story of my faith and its practice of Christian Buddhism. From this aged perspective I see how the writing of my life has always been a reaching to others. From the Nature section comes this dog walking poem:

Grace of the Day

My little dog trots along beside me
treading the street toward the lake.

Late afternoon sun casts shadows
we walk through, without a plan
or worry, moving along like the
gulls above in clear blue skies.

When I stop, she does.
When I start, she begins,
trusting the road and me.
And I trusting her to bring
me home again.

Among the many poems of family this one of fishing with
young Adam echoes much of the truth and wonder of these
sharing times.

Fishing the Lake

What we came for, and what arrives.

My grandson and I walk out the pier
all the way to the lighthouse,
carrying our fishing poles and gear
navigating the huge boulders
that drop off into a deep lake.
*If he falls in, I will follow
unable to live with his loss.*

I bring a bucket of shiners

that we will put back into the lake
two by two, hoping against wind
to draw out a perch or bass,
perhaps a great walleye
to celebrate the day together
in the sun and wind.

The steady hoot of the lighthouse,
the waves washing up on the rocks,
the old guy who shows him
how to bring it in without a snag.
We calculate then cast out,
letting go the line, learning to
sit and wait again and again.

What we came for, and what arrives.

So many of my retirement years after 2003 were spent with and caring for my good friend Bill Wright, an older union organizer and learned man who kept head and heart alive. More than a liberal, he was a progressive in his seeking peace and justice. Personally, he became a friend and second father who unconsciously mentored me in my late 60s. As Bill moved slowly into dementia, he remained a friend to all, his blue blue eyes and warm smile welcoming nurse aides and people in the coffeeshop which he loved. Together with Ann and his close friends we helped Bill through his last years and us into our own.

The Way Home

Sitting in his favorite diner,
again Bill orders what I order,
eggs and bacon with toast.
He tells me of times

he's been here before.

His food grows cold
while I fill my mouth.

His talking is to hang on
to what mind he has left.
He's slipping and knows it...hangs on
...hangs on. The waitress
comes to take our plates,
"Still working on yours, hon?"
"Yes," he says and takes another bite
to prove it to her and himself.
He's telling me how he's
tried reading the paper and
can't make sense of it.
Not just the sentences that
seem to run off, but
the world itself gone astray.

The past is secure, he knows it,
holds it somewhere
in the back rooms of his mind.
Old photos of her start it
like an old car that he once drove
around the block when young.
He hasn't driven for a decade.
He's tried watching tv and
can't follow it either—
the quick turns, threads lost.
He hates this feeling,
losing the way in the coming dark
just wants to get home, to rest,
to fall into her arms and sleep.

And Bill did get his wish in October of 2011 when he passed
on. I was there that day when the hospice choir gathered
around his bed to softly chant him into a peaceful place. He
was on oxygen and could not speak, and yet he moved his
lips to the song.

Finally, *Lake Winds* contains poems of meditation
and of Christian faith, the spirit and soul of my path. Not
exclusionary in any way, I felt the rightness of our group's
Converging Paths title. This is personally expressed in the
long poem that charts my faith journey. Written while I
was taking classes to become a member of the Catholic faith,
"The Journey Home" summarizes much of my faith path:

The Journey Home

I.
Sitting in a front pew of the Potter
Memorial Presbyterian Church,
I wait for my father and uncle
to join me and my brother.
I am 14 years old, a freshman,
and have just come up from
the basement Sunday School.
For long moments I stare up
at the mural painting of Christ
in the Garden of Gethsemane.
In ten minutes the church will almost fill,
and the robed choir will rise slowly to sing,
proclaiming God's love for all.
    "I am weak, but thou art strong.
    Jesus, keep me from all wrong.
    I'll be satisfied as long
    as I walk, dear Lord, close to thee..."
None of this is new to me, yet
something strange is happening here, as I
stare up at Christ kneeling in the garden,

God's light breaking through darkness.
I close my eyes and whisper to myself and God,
> *If you are truly here, God, give me a sign,*
> *make Yourself present to me.*
I am bold yet shaken by this challenge.
At last month's revival, I sat and did
not make the altar call.

The hymn has ended and the minister
stands large before me reading the Gospel.
He raises his arms, extends his open palms
pouring out God's love and grace.
I close my eyes and feel it all
washing over me. A stillness comes to
steal my breath. My body quivers,
my brother moves away. My father
looks down on me sitting there
while others now are standing.
"Are you alright, son?" he asks, and I
shake my head, whisper "I'm going to be sick,"
"Go," he says, "Now." And I do, rushing out
past the others praying the Our Father...
> *Our Father, who art...my father...*

The way home is a blur...past houses and cars,
yards and flowers, up the hill where I
burst through the door, gasping, trembling.
Mother comes towards me from the kitchen,
"What's wrong, honey?" she asks, bending
towards my face. "My God," she sighs,
stroking my hair, "you're whiter than a ghost."
"No, I'm okay," I say and run out and up
the stairs to my room. I throw myself
onto my unmade bed, breathing through tears.
My heart beats strong inside my chest and head.
Love and fear have a hold of me.

I will lie there in God's grace for an hour,
and when I rise, I will tell no one.

II.
Sitting in Brown Chapel at
Muskingum Presbyterian College,
I am humbled by the choir which
rivals even the huge pipe organ
shaking the room into abeyance.
A freshman again, I watch and listen,
afraid of failing my family and class.
Attendance is taken by older peers
as we sit prayerful twice a week.

By midterms, our religious roots
have transplanted to science, math,
literature, and art. Other ways of seeing,
other ways of being. Let them take roll,
we are free to think on our own.
My attention turns to watching co-eds
in the library, smooth legs under
open trench coats. "A small Christian
college for small Christians," someone says,
and one by one we drift outward
onto a lake of doubt or questioning.

III.
Love enters my life, teaching me;
soon Ann and I take classes to wed
in St. Agnes Catholic Church,
sessions with a young priest where
we listen, smile, and nod.
Ann's father walks her down the aisle
in tears, my family sitting on the right side,
unable to kneel at an unfamiliar altar.
We will raise our children in the Church

while they attend public schools. We
compromise our beliefs, and so we sit
as family during mass, I watching the faces
of others take the wafer onto their tongues.

A lover of literature, I read my spiritual light
deep in the Transcendentalists: Emerson and
Thoreau my private saints. Whitman and Dickinson
lights unto themselves. Each summer
I pilgrimage to Concord and Walden Pond
to walk Nature's path under trees of light.

IV.
Now 50 at Mt. Tremper Buddhist Temple
in upstate New York, I *just sit*
staring at wooden floor boards—
bird sounds in the approaching dark.
Stillness fills the room as we walk
mindful of our steps and breath.
In the dark we learn to feel our way
back to our cabins and bunks. Blinded
by our own light, each day we learn
to sit inside the moment, soft breath
of trees and sky. No God to answer to, no
list of sins and commandments,
intuition beyond reason, luminous
from within the space of heart.
Newly awakened I will drive home.

V.
Almost 70 now and retired, a
sitting catholic for 45 years, I
swallow my lack of trust to embrace
the beauty of Christian faith. I rise
from my seat to attend classes,
sense the rich texture of the Word,

the depth of contemplation.
I make a witness before others.
To some I am a convert, to myself
I'm who I've always been, the circle
accepts all faiths of compassion,
grows outward toward infinity.

We still sit with friends in meditation,
welcome others in where more and
more I sense God's grace everywhere
in everything, everyone. The Church
exists imperfect inside the light of God.

At Easter time I take the host and wine
into myself...feel it soften in my mouth
and throat. I am one with it wholly.
Like a salmon swimming back upstream,
I have made the long journey home.

Far from over, this poem statement marks that road I
am on. I continue to both follow and make this path anew
with readings treating Bible scripture of older and newer
Christian and wise Buddhist brothers and sisters. Beside
my seat are books by Christian writers Richard Rohr,
Henri L. Nouen, Thomas Keating, Joan Tollifson, Thomas
Moore, as well as stories of some of the saints—Theresa
and Francis. And with them are books by Buddhist teachers
Tara Bach, Shunryu Suzuki, Pema Chodron, and others.
What seals it for me is finding a writer from one tradition
that does not exclude another. Also, I have met some
wonderful Catholic sisters, Olivia, Pat, Julita, who as
friends have helped me along my spiritual path. More than
anyone else, Ann, so open to spirituality, has been my chief
guide as well as wife and friend. I count myself fortunate
to be in a faith body so deep and rich. If not a leap of faith,

this is at least a release and step off the edge. This poem of our shared and open faith speaks much of our caring and deep bond. I would not be who or where I am on this journey without Ann.

Winter Solstice along the Lake

The sacred scripture of the earth.
—Fionntulach

My wife and I rise at 6 a. m.
and walk the dog down dark streets
in cool lake air, past yards and houses,
lit only by distant streetlamps.

Near the lake we stop to
sense the dark's deep mystery
breathe it in, eyes closed
or open the same.
"Advent time," I feel and say.
"Yes," she whispers back,
"before the birthing of light."
The dog pulls on her leash.

At the shoreline,
our footsteps further the darkness,
as we still, sounds grounding us now,
the quiet roll of the lake's black waters,
our bodies' deep sense of space and time.
And there to the east
above the line of earth
beneath soft hanging clouds
glows a soft purple aura,
maternal curve of light,
the birthing crown.

The dog stills at our feet.
My arms wrap around my wife
as we breathe life's circle,
allow earth's sweet light to come.

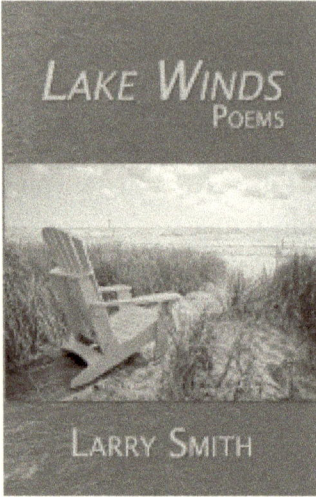

Lake Winds: Poems (2014)   **Author Larry Smith (2010)**

Afterword (2017)

I have joined my wife's group pilgrimage as we trace the spiritual practices of the Pueblo Indian culture of New Mexico. Not a strong believer in mysticism, I remain a full supporter of my wife's interests and recognize its meaning in her life and others. And so I sit with her and forty others on a bus going across the hot desert from Albuquerque on to Amoca Village atop a mesa where we walk and talk with Pueblo people; next day on to Santa Fe and its art and ancient churches; then to Taos and the ancient Pueblo village and people there. At Chimayo, the healing site, we taste blue corn seed, gather a personal stone, share a Catholic Mass, then enter the church's back sacristy where Ann and I bend to touch and taste the earth, rise, then just hold each other close for a long time. Finally the pilgrimage travels to the Bandelier National Parks Monument and its cliff dwellings near Los Alamos. Here, covered in sweat, I will climb the cliff to enter the ancient caves.

The pilgrimage is led by Richard, former priest and spiritual guide, who has given us history and shared stories and rites from Native Americans as well as Catholics, Jews, and Celts. If nothing more, I am one of the accompanying husbands sharing the hot desert weather with Ann and the good company of fellow travelers, each with his or her own faith-belief path.

It is on the return trip to Albuquerque that Richard takes the bus microphone to tell his eye-witnessed story of a woman on their Amazon pilgrimage. In the middle of the jungle she had come down with such severe sciatica pain that she could no longer walk. Her husband grew impatient with the help and demanded they fly in a helicopter to take her to a hospital. "Honestly, I couldn't do that," Richard tells us. "I was stuck for a solution when someone suggested the nearby woman shaman." He tells how the husband scoffed at such witchcraft and voodoo. "But then his wife spoke. She was open to try. And so we carried her to the shaman's hut where the woman looked her over and called for two eggs. 'Bring me two fresh eggs. And hold them to the light to be sure they are fresh.'"

"When the eggs arrived she took one and gently rubbed it all over the woman's body. A hush fell over the room, and then surprising everyone she cracked it over the husband's head." Richard looks up as he says this. "Surprise turned to wonder when a black liquid came streaming out of the egg." We all gasp, as Richard tells us, "And then the woman rose from the stretcher and walked out of the hut." The bus is quiet, then Richard continues in deep sincerity. "I tell you, I was there. I saw this myself." We too feel the wonder as he adds, "Whether healing power or not, it reveals the deep mystery of our body and mind connection."

On our pilgrimage we had done many Pueblo rites, and I had participated in each, though with some degree of doubt. Hearing this story and sensing the sincerity of these others, I reached into my pocket and took hold of my stone. I closed my eyes for a few moments and pressed it tight. What had blind faith in the empirical and doubt in a God brought me? Who was I to cut off the mystery to all this unknown? There is still so much to hold close, to learn from and release. Who wants a life without wonder? Our travels may take us elsewhere, but the journey remains within. I carry that stone with me still and in September will follow the rite of releasing it, casting it out at dusk into our blue Ohio lake.

All life and death are one. The circle expands. The journey continues.

Ann and Larry Smith (c. 2009)

Larry Smith, is a native of the industrial Ohio River Valley having grown up in Mingo Junction, Ohio., the second of four children. His father was a brakeman on the railroad of Weirton Steel where the author worked two summers to help pay for college. A graduate of Mingo High School, Muskingum College, and Kent State University, he taught at Bowling Green State University's Firelands College from 1970 to 2012.

He is the author of eight books of poetry, a previous book of memoirs, five books of fiction, two literary biographies of authors Lawrence Ferlinghetti and Kenneth Patchen, and two books of poetry translations from the Chinese. Smith has received fellowships from the Ohio Arts Council and the National Endowment for the Humanities and was a Fulbright Lecturer in Italy in 1980 to 1981. His photo history of his hometown Mingo Junction appeared in the Images of America Series. Two of his film scripts on authors James Wright and Kenneth Patchen have been made into films with director Tom Koba. He was the first poet laureate of Huron, Ohio.

He is a founder and director of The Firelands Writing Center and a co-founder with his wife of Converging Paths Meditation Center in Sandusky, Ohio. He and wife Ann live along the sandy shores of Lake Erie in Huron, Ohio. They are the parents of three adults and have eight grandchildren.